BRITAIN IN OLD

IS

MELTON MOWBRAY
TO OAKHAM

An old countryman's remark to the author when questioned about the value of publications such as this one.

'Lad! If you don't know where you have come from, you certainly don't know where you are going to!'

A familiar site on the village streets before the Second World War, this steamroller and traction-engine was a most versatile machine. This wood engraving of 1890 illustrates a Wallis and Steeven traction-engine capable of hauling loads of 15 to 20 tons. The front axle could be removed and a roadroller or a pair of wheels attached for ploughing or driving a thrashing drum in a stack-yard.

BRITAIN IN OLD PHOTOGRAPHS

MELTON MOWBRAY TO OAKHAM

TREVOR HICKMAN

SUTTON PUBLISHING LIMITED

First published in 1998 by
Sutton Publishing Limited
Phoenix Mill · Thrupp · Stroud
Gloucestershire · GL5 2BU

**British Library Cataloguing in
Publication Data**
A catalogue record for this book is available
from the British Library.

ISBN 0-7509-2068-8

Cover photographs: *front*: The Cottesmore Hunt leaving
Stapleford Hall, February 1937; *back*: the 3.15 p.m.
Express leaving Wymondham for the east coast holiday
resorts, 1 September 1956.
Title page: John Cooper with Honeysuckle, Teigh, 1964.

By the same author:
Around Melton Mowbray in Old Photographs
Melton Mowbray in Old Photographs
The Vale of Belvoir in Old Photographs
The History of Stilton Cheese
Around Rutland in Old Photographs
East of Leicester in Old Photographs
The Melton Mowbray Album
The History of the Melton Mowbray Pork Pie

Typeset in 10/12 Perpetua.
Typesetting and origination by
Sutton Publishing Limited.
Printed in Great Britain by
Ebenezer Baylis, Worcester.

The arrival of the Stapleford Express at the Lakeside station on the miniature railway at Stapleford Park,
c. 1965. Lord Gretton is at the controls.

CONTENTS

May Day on the showground, now the Sir John Sedley Recreational Field, Wymondham, *c.* 1930.

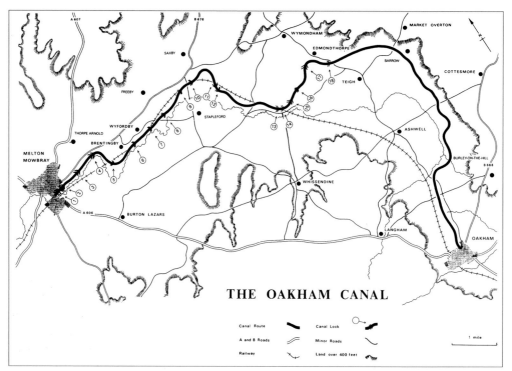

THE OAKHAM CANAL

A plan drawn by David Rogers in 1983, featuring the two towns and most of the villages and hamlets included in this book. It shows the Melton Mowbray to Oakham Canal with its eighteen locks opened in 1802 – the very first barge arrived at Oakham on 16 December that year. Work started on digging the canal in 1795 and by October 1797 it was navigable to Freeby; as the work progressed and the cutting filled with water, so more of the canal became navigable. Because of the obstructive nature of the riparian landowners, there was always a problem with water supply to the canal. A naturally free-flowing river and streams should have been utilized but agreement could not be reached and only limited amounts of water could be drawn off from these sources. What a difference it would have made if the River Eye could have been canalized to and through Stapleford Park. But Lord Harborough, the principal landowner, would not agree to this because it would have ruined his lake and water gardens (*see* pp. 81 and 82).

INTRODUCTION

At first glance the title of this book may seem an odd choice, and the selection of the towns and
villages even more so. There is a reason for it, of course, and in this introduction I will attempt
to clarify my commitment to presenting this book to the reader.

How often do we hear the observation: 'The first half of the twentieth century saw more changes than
any other span of fifty years since records began.' This comment is true. I would suggest that powered
flight allowing man to traverse the globe is the one major single factor in changing the way we live in this
century, opening the world to international travel to everyone who has the means and will to visit foreign
lands. In a different way – but for similar reasons – the development of the canal system of navigational
waterways through the town and villages of England opened up the rural countryside in the nineteenth
century and was part of the Industrial Revolution, which permanently changed the pattern of life in
agricultural England as soon as the system became widespread throughout the country. This change
happened nowhere more so than when the navigation system linked isolated villages to the nearest market
town and to the major areas of population. This book is the story of two towns connected by an industrial
waterway and the villages along its route. It incorporates an account of how change came to a rural area,
along with a photographic record of all the parishes that lie on both banks of the canal.

I first became aware of the Melton Mowbray to Oakham Canal as a small child when gleaning in
cornfields for fallen heads of wheat with my mother during the late 1930s and early 1940s. As a
lunchtime relaxation I traversed the banks of the dried-up bed of the canal by Cord Hill near
Wymondham Roughs. Further exploration of the derelict waterway took place with my father and friends
searching for moorhens' eggs in springtime during the 1940s: these were a delicacy when fried and
became a regular Sunday morning breakfast during the years of the Second World War.

The coming of the canal to high Leicestershire and Rutland would have been just as dramatic to the
people of the nineteenth century as the news that Alcock and Brown had flown the Atlantic was to my
father and mother. Horizons had suddenly expanded; the towns of Melton Mowbray and Oakham were
no longer isolated and the villages were never again to be considered islands in the fields.

For the greater part of 800 years little or no change had taken place in village life. Politics may have
changed at national level and religious life certainly changed but the everyday business of the 'common
man' had changed very little – birth, living, working, establishing a home and dying in the isolated
villages of this part of England. In my youth, working as a farm labourer was the normal occupation for a
man as it had been for over 1,000 years. They were referred to over the centuries as serfs, villeins,
sokemen, borders, labourers and farm workers. But whether a man was a plain slave to the lord of the
manor, a labourer or an individual liable for tithes and taxes to the overlord and to the church, he relied
upon the land for his living.

Prior to the coming of the waterways, the main all-weather system for transporting goods between isolated villages was pack-horse or pack-horse train. In addition wagons would have been used during the summer months but when rain fell the use of wheeled vehicles would have been seriously curtailed. When they were running, the wagons or carriers' carts occasionally carried passengers and of course always had a wide variety of goods for sale at the local market. The carrier would make some purchase on behalf of his village customers for delivery on the return journey. Very little trade would be in bulk orders, the exception being stone for speciality structures such as churches and for use as quoins on the manor house or vicarage. Whenever possible these stones were transported by water using rafts on the local rivers and streams. Roads could only be used for such transport during the summer months when pack-horse trains could carry the stone in wicker panniers.

The arrival of the canal did not bring about instant change but the navigation system did make it possible to move larger quantities of goods in one load, and it brought 'foreigners' to the town and village. The navvies, canal workers, traders, dealers and other ancillary workers who widened trade and commerce all came to the area, and so began the movement of people to and from the industrial centres of England.

The canals had an impact on other aspects of life too. Before they came all villages were self-sufficient, wages more often than not being paid in kind – cash was of little use to the average farm worker: where could he go to spend it? Most cottages were constructed from wattle-and-daub with thatched roofs, and local stone would only have been used on the more important features such as the chimney breast and stack and possibly as foundation supports in better class cottages. Of course the manor house, the church, possibly the vicarage and certain barns that were used to store the tithe were often constructed totally from locally quarried stone. But to the east of Melton Mowbray there would have been no slate or tiled roofs, little or no brickwork; in fact none of the labourers' cottages would have been constructed with sound foundations. In those wattle-and-daub cottages that survived into the nineteenth century the deteriorating infill mix of twigs, mud, sand, lime, cow hair, etc. was replaced with stone along the floor level, thus supporting the rotten ends of the main beams that had been set into the sub-soil. Later bricks were placed, often in herringbone fashion, between the horizontal and cross beams. These beams were in the main crudely trimmed ash branches although some oak was used. Ash was the main timber used on the smaller beams; it could be used green because of its ease of splitting and low sap content.

The roofs were thatched with straw or local reeds and ten years would be a fair lifespan; because of the nature of the materials and the crudity of house construction, if a cottage lasted longer than a decade it was a miracle. The wattle and daub dwellings were normally 'cruck built', two trees forming an arch at either end of the building with supporting walls made of branches and twigs which supported the crude plaster coating. A cottage would be constructed in a matter of days using communal labour. Many were nothing more than 'barns' with a loft above the main room. The fire used for heating would be in the middle of the cottage, the smoke finding its way out through a hole in the thatch. It does not take much imagination to realize what would happen after a few dry summers when the sparks were rising from an open fire on to a dry thatched roof during the winter gales!

The canals changed all this and brought new building technology to the countryside. Tile and brick making arrived because canals require locks and millions of bricks were needed to construct both them and bridges along the canal; most were made from clay excavated locally and fired near the cuttings. Roof tiles also arrived with the new development and so village life changed – the constant fear of fire and the total destruction of homes no longer haunted village families.

The waterways arrived in this area of the East Midlands at a time of great economic upheaval, the dawn of the Industrial Revolution, and their development meant communication between villages and towns reached a standard that had not been experienced since the time of the Roman occupation. The situation did not change completely, however, and many Leicestershire people remained cut off by modern standards well into the twentieth century. I have had contact in the past with village people who had never visited London and only on two or three occasions visited Leicester, our county town, during their lifetime. It was considered an occasion to visit Melton Mowbray market once a month on a Tuesday. People never expected anything else during their life in the village community. Today restrictions that meant a person would be born and would die in a village (certainly this would apply to most females), and only visit the local market town three or five times in a lifetime would now be most intolerable. If you were fit, a walk of 7 miles to market and back during the summer months was acceptable. Many men would do this but for the farm labourer's wife, permanently pregnant, this would be impossible; a second-class citizen, she was subjected to a lifetime of servitude and had an average life expectancy of some twenty odd years. Her husband would be lucky to reach thirty-five. Change had to come for the lower-working-class farm worker.

Joseph Morley sheep shearing near the pinfold at Teigh, 1929. Standing in the pinfold behind the fence to the left is a cottage constructed with mud/clay walls; the roof is thatched with straw. This was almost certainly the pinfold keeper's cottage, a medieval construction of considerable antiquity. This cottage was not unique; there would have been thousands of such constructions scattered across the countryside for possibly nearly 2,000 years. Farm workers' cottages constructed from free local materials left no trace for the modern archaeologist when they fell into disuse and collapsed. The walls, the roof and timber supports decayed and were absorbed into the earth from whence they came. It is a tragedy that this cottage was allowed to fall down in the 1950s.

The change to this way of life which began with the canal continued in the 1840s with the introduction of the railways, and of course changes are with us still. In this area of England we now have the commuter village. The village life of the eighteenth century has long gone. Nineteenth-century England still lingers in isolated pockets in some villages, but in the main the delightful 'picture postcard' villages situated between Melton Mowbray and Oakham are now commuter villages. A fine system of roads and the modern reliable motor car are responsible for this. I do not consider that this is wrong. We live in a changing world and no one wants eighteenth-, nineteenth- or, for that matter, early twentieth-century village life to return with its awful problems of hygiene that were part of everyday life. On average we all live longer now and those who are fortunate to live in such a delightful area of England should be grateful. Village and town life has changed dramatically since the Melton Mowbray to Oakham Canal was dug through the low hills and valley that are spread out between these two towns. Newcomers to a village in particular are always treated with some suspicion by their neighbours, often by people who have lived in the area themselves for only a few years. No matter how long you have lived in a village or town, at some time you or your family were newcomers. In my case, my family arrived in this area in 1745 as farmers on the Sherrard estate, perhaps as a result of an eviction. Were they welcomed with open arms? I doubt it!

Villages and towns are about people. In this book there are many photographs of landscape views. Without exception all these views are man-made, so this book is about people and the landscape. I have compiled it around the theme of change; in my opinion the big leap forward began at the end of the eighteenth century and is still with us. I mention early history when I consider it is relevant. This book is not a complete record – no one person could produce such a volume. The Victoria County History is attempting this task; the Leicestershire series has yet to be completed and Rutland is complete, though even in these excellent publications much is missed. I present this collection of facts and photographs as an addition to all that has been published and trust it will be of interest to all those who browse through its pages.

The collection of pictures in this book, and the potted history of a delightful area of eastern England which goes with it, complements my two previous books on the area – The Melton Mowbray Album and Around Rutland. The photographs selected have been chosen as an attempt to record much that has happened in the two towns and villages since the turn of the nineteenth century. The majority have not previously been published in book form. I have included extended captions, especially where photographs and engravings present a picture of important events that have taken place in the area, some of national interest, one – the famous fight at Thistleton Gap – of international importance. This has been my 'home patch' for over sixty years and I consider it is 'Forever England'!

Trevor Hickman
Wymondham, June 1998

CHAPTER ONE

LEICESTERSHIRE

In the introduction to this book considerable emphasis is placed on the construction of the canal from Melton Mowbray to Oakham. A waterway such as this radically altered the way heavy goods like coal, bricks, tiles, lime, etc. were transported. But another way of transporting goods existed before the canals were built and continued long after many were closed – the local carrier's cart. In this photograph we see Walter Skerritt standing near Robert Gresham's carrier's cart on a highway somewhere in east Leicestershire in 1910. Gresham was a baker who ran his business at 10 Pall Mall, off Bentley Street, and Norman Street in Melton Mowbray. As a retailer visiting the villages around Melton Mowbray with his cart, he would convey goods back to town after his bread deliveries had been made.

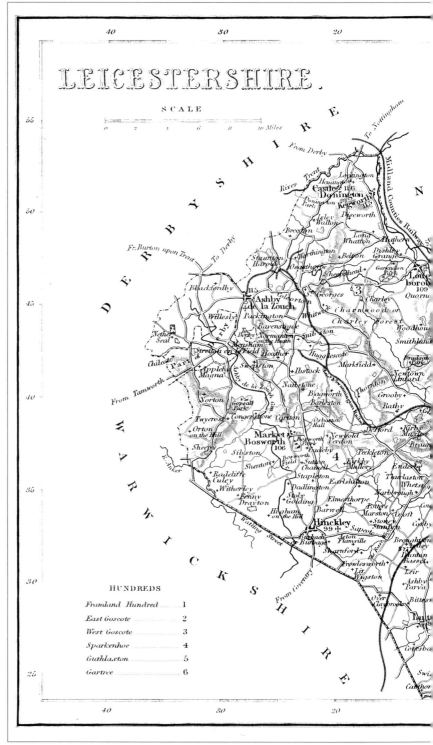

A map of Leicestershire published in 1842 by J. Archer, and including very interesting information for the industrial archaeologist. The turnpike roads were still in use, canals and navigable waterways criss-crossed the county and the railway

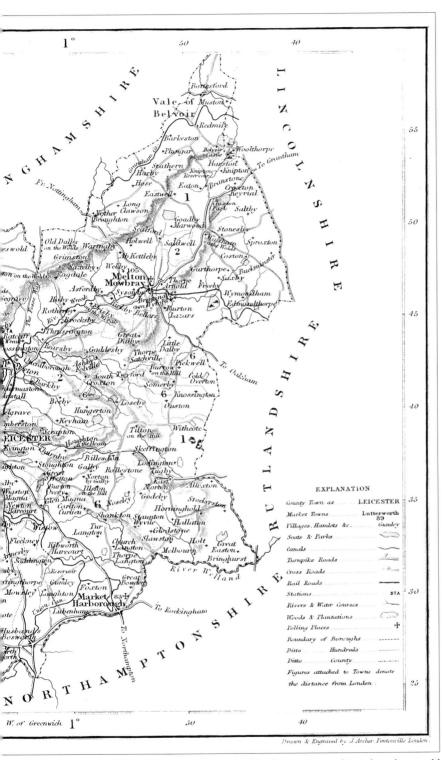

system was just being constructed. Considerable changes were taking place that would have been welcomed by many people but feared by others.

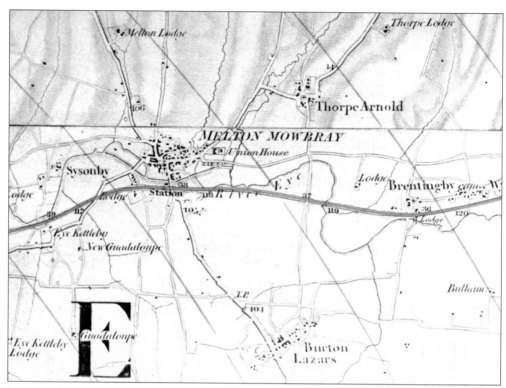

Section of the 1835 edition of the Ordnance Survey, revised in 1867. It is difficult to say how accurate this map is. Alterations were made by erasing the engraving on the metal plate and then re-engraving the changes. The Melton Mowbray to Oakham Canal has been erased from the fields to the east of Melton Mowbray, although interestingly it is still clearly marked as far as the stream that runs from Thorpe Arnold and feeds into the River Eye. This area was developed for industry and the production of gas from coal (see the gasholders in the photograph opposite). Presumably until the railway was fully operational, coal was still delivered along the Leicester to Melton navigations to the coking ovens. The detail from the plan (below) drawn by Stephen Fry in about 1850 shows the gasworks.

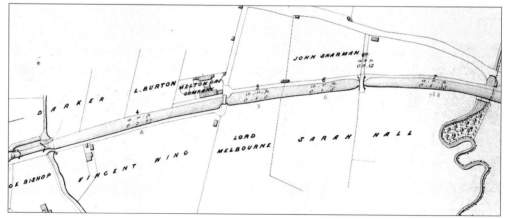

CHAPTER TWO

MELTON BOROUGH

This aerial photograph of Melton Mowbray was taken before 1928, the year that work started on building Wilton Road and that part of Egerton Lodge was demolished. The foreground shows High Street still connecting into Leicester Street. In the background the two gasholders off Saxby Road are clearly visible standing near to the Wyvern Knitting Wool Spinning Mill, then owned by T.W. Rust & Co. and now Pedigree Petfoods factory. The site of tennis courts off Leicester Road was still open fields.

THE NAVIGATION

In 1881 the basin that served the Melton Mowbray Navigation and the canal to Oakham was filled in. Opened in 1795, it closed for traffic on 1 August 1877, thirty years after the Melton to Oakham Canal had closed. This photograph was possibly taken in the late 1890s and shows the canal and tow-path running from the Play Close to Leicester Road. A barrier had been erected to prevent boats entering the Play Close area. The photographer stood in the Play Close. The iron bridge still stands and swimming baths have since been built on the land behind the bridge.

Canalization of the River Eye, 1935. This canal cutting was made to avoid the bend in the river in front of Egerton Lodge for two reasons: first for ease of transport; but above all to keep canal traffic away from the front of the stately home. The waterway shown connects with the canal under the bridge detailed in the photograph above.

MELTON MOWBRAY RAILWAY STATIONS

Melton Mowbray Town station, Thursday 1 January 1959. A railway station was opened on 1 September 1846 on this site off Burton Street. In this photograph an LMS Standard Class 2 express is just entering the station. This was the daily express from Yarmouth to Leicester. Two months later the east coast Midland and Great Northern line from Norfolk via Edmondthorpe and Wymondham station was closed down. In the foreground the station porter Jim Hatton is talking to an inspector from Derby.

A Class B1 4–6–0 engine from the Colwick shed, passing through Melton Mowbray North station in July 1962 pulling the Leicester (Belgrave Road) excursion to Skegness on the LNW/GNR joint line from Welham Junction near Market Harborough to Bottesford. This railway station off Scalford Road was opened on 1 September 1879 and closed to passenger traffic in December 1953. Note the unusual cantilever signal box to the left of the photograph.

PAINTING THE TOWN RED

On Thursday 6 April 1837 the town of Melton Mowbray entered into the folklore of England because of an escapade that took place at around three o'clock in the morning. Much has been written about this act of vandalism. Any group of people who are in high spirits through strong drink and are supposedly enjoying themselves are said to be 'painting the town red' and indeed in Melton Mowbray revellers once really did. The sorry affair started at Croxton Park races on 5 April 1837 when the Marquess of Waterford and numerous friends consumed too much wine and began making their way home by carriage and on horseback. It is presumed they arrived at the Thorpe End tollgate at the junction of the Grantham and Saxby Road. They found the gates shut and a confrontation took place with the gatekeeper. Did they refuse to pay the toll? Whatever the case they certainly decided to take action. Repair work was taking place on the property, and they took some tools and screwed up the windows and doors. It would seem there was also considerable red paint on site; this they daubed over the house and gates. The gatekeeper attempted to fire his pistol at the revellers. It misfired because it was incorrectly charged and this attracted the town constables who were immediately set upon by the unruly mob of 'gentlemen'. They proceeded down the Beast Market (Sherard Street) painting doors and windows red, before arriving at the White Swan in the Market Place. The Marquess was hoisted up on to the carved swan and proceeded to paint it red as depicted (above left) in the engraving by Henry Alken. The post office, banks, shops and private homes suffered from the paint too and had their windows screwed up. Proceeding down Burton Street, the vandals then removed the sign from the Red Lion public house that stood next to the Harborough Hotel and threw it into the canal. By this time the watch and many constables had been alerted, and attempts at arresting the culprits were made. One, Edward Reynard, was apprehended. He was lodged in the Bridewell (prison) on King Street. This enraged the Marquess who, with Sir Frederick Johnstone and others, laid siege to the prison, breaking down the doors and beating up the constables who were forced to release Reynard. The following day the town was in uproar; summonses were issued. The culprits were finally brought to trial one year later at Derby Assize Court, on Tuesday 31 July 1838, on a charge of causing a riot. All were found not guilty but were fined £100 each on a charge of assault. Privately Lord Waterford had ensured that well in advance of the trial everyone who had suffered distress as a result of the escapade was adequately recompensed for the damage caused and for the group's behaviour.

FLOODS

With the building of locks and diversion of watercourses, construction of a navigable waterway unquestionably brought about flooding in the area around Melton Mowbray. The Oakham Canal Company was sued in 1838 for flooding the Saxby Road at Swing Bridge, still an area prone to flooding, and the various locks and sluices held back the flow of water from Leicester. Many serious floods have taken place over the last one hundred and fifty years. Possibly the worst took place on August Bank Holiday Monday 1922: violent thunderstorms moved stacked hayricks from the meadows and clogged culverts, bridges and above all the lock gates at Rhubarb Island, Sysondby. This photograph shows Albert Hyde on horseback rescuing a cow from drowning, pulling it up Burton Street for Harry Beeby, who is the horseman wearing the bowler hat. Albert worked for Harry as his stockman.

Seventy-six years later possibly the second-worst flood of the twentieth century took place in Melton Mowbray on Good Friday 10 April 1998. This photograph, taken in the Play Close, is of the traditional Easter Fair flooded out. At the height of the flood parts of Burton Street, Brook Street and other areas were inundated with over 3 ft of water.

PORK PIES & HUNT CAKE

Pork pies have been made in and around Melton Mowbray for centuries, principally because of the development of the Stilton cheese industry in the area which creating vast quantities of surplus whey, a superb cheap pig food. In this photograph Stephen Hallam is hand-raising the pastry case for a Melton Mowbray pork pie in Dickinson & Morris's famous bakery on Nottingham Street, Melton Mowbray, where pies were first made in 1851. See *The History of the Melton Mowbray Pork Pie*.

The making-up of the world famous Melton Hunt cake which has been created exclusively at Dickinson & Morris bakery at Melton Mowbray from the finest natural ingredients since 1854. A cake selected and enjoyed by the fox-hunters of Melton Mowbray in the nineteenth century, it matures well and can be posted throughout the world by the makers from this Nottingham Street shop. Eric Turner is levelling the slab cake in wooden frames, Dawn Sanson is adding cherries and toasted almonds, and Tony Wensley is placing the cake mix into hoops.

MELTON MARKET

Established for over a thousand years, Melton Mowbray Tuesday market is as viable as it ever was. Many of the thoroughfares have now been pedestrianized. This scene of the market in front of the White Swan porch was taken at the turn of the twentieth century but it could be repeated on the streets throughout the centre of the town today.

A photograph contemporary with the one printed above, showing the Market Place at the turn of the century. The youths are standing in front of Fred Warner's pork pie and confectionery shop. Note the cobbled thoroughfare that stretches out into the highway.

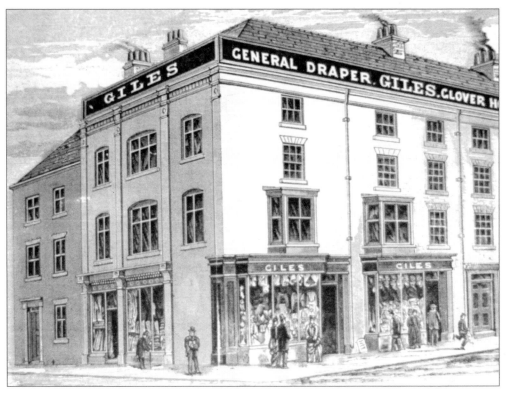

Wood engraving of Giles & Middletons, draper's, milliner's, etc., 20 Market Place, 1892. This was part of 'The Barnes Block', long since demolished to increase the area for the weekly market.

The west side of the Market Place, 1892. From left to right: no. 20, Giles & Middleton; no. 21, Felix Gamble, hatter, hosier, shirtmaker etc.; no. 27, William Willcox, draper; no. 28, Jonathan Towne, printer, bookseller, agent for the Norwich Fire & Life Assurance Co.; no. 29, Wing & Son, proprietor George N. Wing, chemist and grocer.

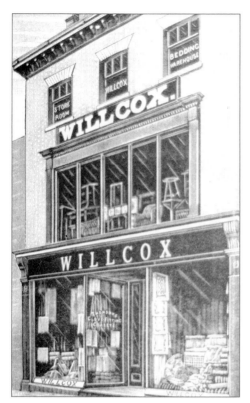

A wood engraving used as an advertisement for Willcox draper's, 27 Market Place, clearly showing items that are offered for sale, 1892.

Wing's chemist's and grocer's, 29 Market Place, 1892. A few years later Towne's moved to this property. When they vacated it, WH Smith's purchased the building and still occupies the premises.

William Bowley & Co. in 'The Barnes Block', Market Place, 1936. Established in the nineteenth century as a watchmaker's, the business expanded to become the town's leading jeweller's under the direction of William Katz.

BEER & SPIRITS

Langton & Sons Thorpe End brewery in a wood engraving, 1892. In this illustration a horse and cart are being led from the cartshed on the right. The building was demolished in 1910 and The Pavilion was built on the site; in July 1911 it opened as a music-hall known as The Palace. In 1912 a foyer was added, a licence was granted to run film shows and it became Melton Mowbray's first permanent cinema. Now it is Central Wool Grower's warehouse and the foyer has been demolished.

A wood engraving of King Street House used as an advertisement for William Albert Heap, wine and spirit merchant of 3 King Street, 1892.

DIAMOND JUBILEE

In 1897 considerable celebrations took place throughout the British Isles for the diamond jubilee of Queen Victoria. This photograph was taken on Nottingham Street as the parade was passing. William Lowe's plumber's shop is at no. 6.

Melton town notables leading the parade down Nottingham Street during the celebrations for Queen Victoria's diamond jubilee. They are passing John Robert Wartnaby & Co., furniture dealer, at nos 10–11.

TOWN ESTATE

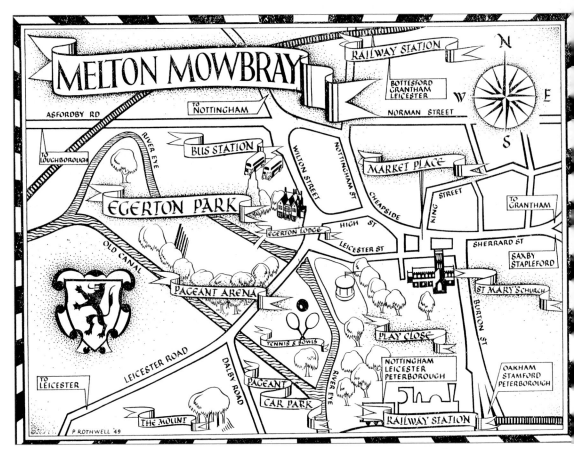

During Whit week 1949 celebrations took place throughout Melton Mowbray to mark 400 years since the formation of the Town Estate. The author had just left school and has vivid memories of making up and stapling together the eighty-page programme of events that was printed by J.W. Warner & Son of 2 South Parade to support the week-long pageant. The above plan was printed in the programme.

The Town Estate was formed when a group of townspeople purchased a property known as The Spytell Chapell in 1549. This was religious guild land, requisitioned for the Crown in 1547 and sold to William Gyles who in turn sold it to Christopher Draper. It was finally purchased by Nicholas Collyshaw on behalf of the inhabitants of Melton Mowbray. From this first purchase other lands were obtained and the estate controlled some of the common land, making a charge for tethering and tenting of cattle. As the years rolled by officers were appointed for various duties – town wardens, herdsmen and swine herdsmen (pigs have always figured large in stock management in the area), crowscarers, bridgemasters, overseers of pavements, constables, schoolmasters, clock-keepers, to name only some.

During the reign of Queen Elizabeth I the twelve feofees (the elected managers) were responsible for the town armoury that was held at the White Swan in the Market Place. They also had to ride out to the village of Buckminster to maintain the beacon which was lit to warn Belvoir Castle when the Spanish Armada was approaching, part of a system of beacons stretching throughout the British Isles.

Until local governments were formed the Estate took care of the town. In 1850, after considerable negotiations with Lord Melbourne, the lord of the manor, the Estate purchased the manorial rights and the right to collect market tolls. Spital Leys is still owned by the Estate; it is the site of the Cattle Market off of Scalford Road. The Estate also owns other considerable areas of land including the Play Close at Egerton Park. In 1999 it will celebrate 450 years as a charitable institution.

A group of 'crusaders' who took part in Episode Two, 'The Lords of Melton 1160–94', of the pageant held on Egerton Park, Whit week 1949.

Halberd Bearers for the Town Estate, 1936. Left to right: G. Harwood, G. Chambers, H. Peach.

G. Irving BA, Pageant Master for the Melton Mowbray Town Estate, Whit week, 1949.

LEICESTER ROAD BRIDGE

Leicester Road bridge was built in 1822, replacing a seven-arched bridge that was situated a few yards further to the west. The fields to the east had yet to be developed into the Town Estate's tennis courts. This photograph was taken in around 1905.

The Town Estate began to develop the playing fields to the east of the Leicester Road bridge some years after the photograph at the top of this page was taken. A tree-planting programme was got under way. An interesting comparison can be made when visiting the site today. Fully matured trees now overhang the bridge.

BURTON END

No book containing old photographs of Melton Mowbray would be complete without a view of Anne of Cleves house. This one was taken in around 1906 shows Anne's house on the left. Henry Reynolds' milliner's shop is at the end of Burton End with the series of steps leading up to his premises. Lamberts Lane is to the right, leading to Sherrard Street. Reynolds' shop was demolished in 1911 to widen Burton End. The whole road is now called Burton Street.

An equally interesting building on Burton End/Street is the Bede Houses; this photograph of the rear of the property was taken in 1892. The houses were built to house poor people in 1646 as a result of an endowment by Robert Hudson in 1638.

PLAY CLOSE

Melton Mowbray Town Estate purchased the land to lay out a park in 1866 for £670. This photograph, possibly taken at the turn of the twentieth century, shows the recently erected bandstand and the line of newly planted trees.

Further land was purchased in 1872 by the Town Estate to extend the Play Close. This photograph taken in the 1920s shows the tennis court laid out in the open fields at the left of the picture at the top of page 28.

PARADES: MELTON

Church parade for the memorial service for King Edward VII, 20 May 1910. A much-loved monarch, he frequented Melton Mowbray for the fox-hunting and to meet the fast-living wealthy socialites, among whom were some of his known thirteen mistresses. He established the Entente Cordiale with France and did much to help the working populace of Great Britain. His sudden death from bronchitis was felt keenly by all strata of society. At the rear of this photograph are Fred and Joe Brewin.

British Legion Armistice parade leaving Sage Cross Street for Sherrard Street, 1919. Malcolm Sargent conducted the town band on this occasion.

HOME GUARD

Dad's Army, the BBC comedy programme, has done much to publicize the Home Guard in England. According to Daphne Toulson who produced this cartoon in 1943, the series is a fair representation of what actually went on. Her father Major Arthur Percival Marsh – A.P.M. to his friends – lies behind the tree stump wearing the peaked cap. Sunday afternoon was the time for manoeuvres: 'it's a miracle nobody was killed,' according to Daphne. There was no lack of enthusiasm in Melton Mowbray. The mind was willing, but because of age the body often let the part-time defence volunteers down!

Weekend camps were a source of enjoyment for many old soldiers recruited into the Home Guard. This photograph was taken on August Bank Holiday Monday, 1941. Melton Mowbray Home Guard was at camp in Denton Park, near Grantham, Lincolnshire. Left to right: -?-, Frank Warner, Mr Gates (Barclay's Bank Manager), -?-.

The final parade of the Melton Mowbray Home Guard, led by their CO Major A.P. Marsh OBM, 1945. They are taking their last salute on Wilton Road. Major Marsh served as a Captain in the 5th Leicestershire Regiment during the First World War. In 1943 he was awarded the Order of the British Empire (Military) for his service to the defence corps.

A.P.M. by Bert Gerry, the famous cartoonist, who worked for the *Melton Mowbray Times* in the 1930s and early '40s. Arthur Percival Marsh was the senior partner at Oldham Marsh, Solicitors, Registrar for Melton Mowbray, County Councillor, and Clerk to the Melton and Belvoir Rural District Council. In addition to these positions he undertook many other civic duties.

SAS

1 Troop, 2nd SAS Regiment at Gartre, Sandy Lane, Melton Mowbray, 1944. This photograph was taken quite illegally at the home of Captain Michael Marsh MC who is the troop commander sitting in the centre of the front row of the Special Air Service soldiers. Marsh was commissioned into the 9th Queens Royal Lancers (Mechanised) as a Second Lieutenant at the age of twenty-two and was posted to the western desert where he was promoted to Lieutenant. He was in command of B Squadron in an action in El Hamma and led his men in an attack on a well-fortified enemy position, capturing 88mm and 50mm guns. For his part in this attack he was awarded the MC. After this incident he was seconded to the SAS under the command of the founder of this élite regiment, Colonel David Stirling. Marsh saw action with the SAS behind enemy lines at the Battle of El Alamein and is listed as a serving Lieutenant, A Squadron, in Virginia Cowles' famous book *The Phantom Major* (1958). After Colonel Stirling's capture by the enemy the SAS regiment was enlarged and dispersed to take part in the invasion of Italy and France. Marsh was promoted to Captain and returned to England to train an élite troop to be dropped by parachute into occupied Europe. Early in 1944 Marsh was detailed to train his troop in subversive actions behind enemy lines by infiltrating a Midlands airfield, marking planes as destroyed on the runway, and returning to base without being observed. It is thought that the airfield was Cottesmore. Travelling by night and hiding during the day they successfully 'attacked' the airfield, much to the annoyance of the regiment guarding the base who said this could not be done. Marsh's name was leaked and the regiment made a night raid on his Melton Mowbray home. It was a correct decision because he was certainly at home, but he and the whole troop were hidden in the roof space. A watch was maintained on the front of the house but Marsh and his men got away by removing tiles from the roof, climbing down the rainwater pipes and heading across the fields to base, undetected. Shortly after this escapade Marsh was parachuted into France with his men; he and his troops joined forces with the Maquis. They carried out many successful raids, including blowing up the railway system and thereby helping the D-Day landings. Captain Marsh's code name while in France was 'Jo Jo'. Being on active service in France assisting the resistance movement was an unbelievably dangerous mission. In action death was always a very real possibility. If an SAS soldier was captured while he was with a resistance fighter, he was immediately executed by the Gestapo; this happened to a number of very brave members of the regiment. After France was liberated Captain Marsh was dropped into Germany where he undertook many subversive acts and remained undetected, living off the land until Germany surrendered. After he was demobbed he joined the Leicestershire Yeomanry TA and was promoted to Major. He died tragically in a house fire at Burton Lazars in January 1983.

SIR FRANCIS GRANT

The Lodge off Dalby Road, Melton Mowbray, 1906. This was the home of Sir Francis Grant from 1841 until he died there on 5 October 1878. He was elected President of the Royal Academy in March 1866 and knighted the same year. His family declined the honour of his being buried in Westminster Abbey and he was laid to rest in St Mary's Close, off Norman Way.

Lord Howth and Francis Grant taking a five barred gate by Francis Grant, 1825. Undoubtedly his most famous work is *The Melton Breakfast*. He painted two versions, the first during the reign of William IV, and they were subsequently issued as large, engraved, hand-coloured prints (*see The Melton Mowbray Album*, p. 18).

CHINA COLLECTABLES

Today tourism plays a most important part in the economy of any historic shire town and Melton Mowbray is no exception. Who were the first tourists? The eighteenth-century fox-hunters could be classed as such. They took cheese and pies when they returned to the capital, and some took more permanent mementoes such as this pill box. Produced from very thin china supported by fine brass rimming, it has been photographed next to a modern 5 pence piece, and was possibly constructed to contain a strong drug in pill form.

When Adolphus Goss began marketing his crested china in the 1870s, much interest was generated in producing fine porcelain objects such as this cockerel by Swan China, a typical present to take home from a visit to Melton Mowbray cattle market in the 1920s.

An anvil by Arcadian, a Stoke-on-Trent pottery firm that began producing fine china ornaments soon after Goss pieces became popular. (*See The History of the Melton Mowbray Pork Pie*, p. 55.)

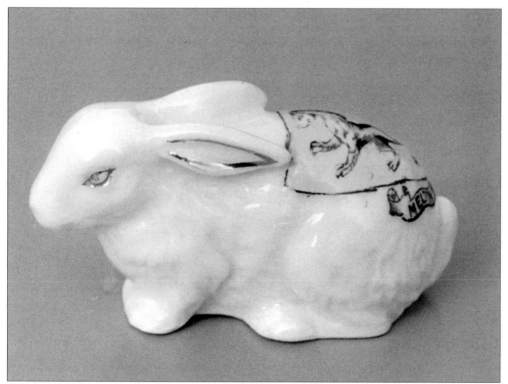

Melton market sells poultry and rabbits as well as cattle, sheep and horses. Also a lively trade existed between about 1920 and 1945 in selling braces of shot wild rabbits by auction. If a sportsman had a good day at the market obtaining good prices for his kills, he could have purchased this crested china rabbit by Arcadian to take home to his wife as a celebration.

CARNEGIE LIBRARY

The Carnegie Free Library on Thorpe End, Melton Mowbray, *c.* 1910. Now the town museum, opened in 1977, this library was built mainly through the unstinting efforts of William Willcox. William was born at Kneeton, Nottinghamshire, on 18 August 1844; his parents were related to the Day family of Wymondham and as a child he lived for a short time in that village. In October 1853 his mother, a widow, moved to Melton Mowbray where William was educated by the Vicar of St Mary's church, Dr William Morris Colles. After finishing his education he was apprenticed to J.F. Gibson, a draper, in the Market Place and in due course he opened his own business (*see* engraving on p. 23). As a result of inheritance passed down from the wealthy Day family of Wymondham, he was reasonably financially secure: in the 1873 land survey he owned just over 55 acres and had an estimated annual income from rents of £203. William married Mary Barnes on 22 April 1869, the service being conducted by Dr Colles. William was churchwarden, sidesman and Sunday School teacher at St Mary's. A founder director of the Melton Mowbray Building Society and Feoffee of the Town Estate, he was the main driving force behind obtaining money from the Carnegie Foundation to build the free library. He laid the foundation stone with a silver trowel on 21 July 1904; one year on, on the 26 October 1905, he was invited to perform the ceremonial opening. William retired from business in the autumn of 1904 and lived in Bottesford. He passed away on 23 January 1906. A portrait of him hung for years in the Carnegie Library and is now in Melton Mowbray County Library on Wilton Road; an inscription placed under the painting states: 'The Father of the Town'.

THE BELL HOTEL

The Bell Hotel on Nottingham Street, *c.* 1910. The sign above the doorway reads 'accommodation for motorists'. A typical Georgian building constructed specifically for the coaching trade, it never obtained the level of business that its near neighbour, The George on High Street, did. The Bell was enlarged in the 1870s and its heyday was when it was used by the fox-hunters visiting the town at the turn of the century. For some years it was the headquarters of the Conservative Party and election candidates would address the crowd from the bay window above the door.

Compare the entrance to the stables to the Bell on this photograph with the one printed above. In the earlier photograph the entrance is curved and high to accommodate horse-drawn coaches; a lowered, squared, entrance was big enough for the cars which had taken over as transport by the time this photograph was taken in the 1960s.

MELTON TRADERS

Melton Mowbray Rotary Club, 1936. Most of the leading businessmen of Melton Mowbray in the 1930s are in this formal group. Back row, left to right: W.E. Katz, A. Scarborough, J.E. Brownlow, J. Litchfield, P.C. Shelbourne. Middle row: A.H. Crane, F. Shouler, D.S. Hayes, F.E. Warner, C.R. Crasher, W. Rowell, P.D. Prior, E.P. Sentence. Front row: W.E. Warnes, R. Stuart-Smith, A.P. Marsh, J. Green, H.K. Barker, R.W. Brownlow, Canon Robson, Dr M. Dixon, R.F. Skinner.

Frank Warner with Miss Micklewight in front of J.W. Warner's, 2 South Parade, c. 1905.

Wood engraving of Sharman & Ladbury's premises at 36 Sherard Street, 1892. At this time they were silversmiths, ironmongers and agricultural implement makers.

A caricature of W.E. (Bill) Warner by Bert Gerry published in the *Melton Times*,1938. Bill Warner ran the pork pie shop in the Market Place; his trade mark was his 'pork pie hat'.

Sam Garner, ironmonger and agricultural engineer, of Garner & Sons, 7 Cheapside, 1936.

Henry Robert Milner, chemist, 6 Cheapside, 1892. This business was eventually purchased by R.W. Brownlow.

Ellis & Everard staff loading coal direct from the railway wagons in the Melton Mowbray station sidings, off Burton Street, 1936.

C.B. Payne of the highly reputable furnisher's on High Street, 1936.

R.W. Snelson of the Melton Mowbray Building Society, 1936.

SPORTING OCCASIONS

Melton Mowbray Amateurs Football Club 1901/2. Back row, left to right: F. Warner, Tompkins, Morris, Cragg, C. Bingham, Bottom, S. Farrow. Front row: Goodacre, Gilian, R. Smith, T. Moorhouse, J. Poyzer, J. Gamble.

Gala Day at the Swan's Nest swimming pool in the River Eye, off Saxby Road, 1936. This pool was at the edge of the River Eye where it runs along the boundary of Petfoods Sports Ground.

Staff and students of Melton Mowbray Grammar School who took part in a play by J.M. Barrie during the academic year 1935/6. Back row, left to right: Peggy Graham, Betty Lovell, Eric Bruce, Peggy Warr, Ken Lounds, Daphne Mountain, Eric Fensome, Diane Fletcher. Middle row: Marjorie Bramley, Joyce Barnes, Kelvin Chadfield, Jill Simmons, Mr Entwistle (English master), Kath Beaver, -?-, Janet Payne, Pippa Warner. Front row: Margery Lowe, -?-, -?-, -?-, -?-, -?-.

Thorpe Road paddling pool, 1936. This provided endless fun for the children of the area during the long hot summers of the 1930s and '40s. It was situated across the stream in the field to the left of the present road leading to Tesco's and has long since been filled in in the name of hygiene.

Revellers at the British Legion Ball held in the Corn Exchange, 1936. In this group are the President General J. Vaughan and Mrs Vaughan, Captain and Mrs Burns Hartopp, Captain A.P. and Mrs Marsh, Ted and Mrs Garner, Dick and Mrs Brewit.

The Marsh family at the Memorial Hospital Ball, 1936. Back, left to right: Michael Marsh (*see* p. 34), Arthur Percival Marsh (*see* p. 32). Front: Adine Marsh, Daphne Marsh.

THORPE ARNOLD

Copper engraving of Thorpe Arnold church in 1793 from a drawing by J. Pridden.

Thorpe Arnold church and vicarage in 1913 when Revd Walter Lechmere Tudor BA was in residence.

Corfe, the fine Victorian home of Mr and Mrs William Bowley, Thorpe Arnold, 1906.

The height of the big freeze, 23 February 1947. Left to right: Silence Holmes, Jack Holmes and Ethel Holmes on the Waltham Road, near Thorpe Arnold (*see* p. 39).

PEPPERMINT BILLY

A nineteenth-century engraving of Thorpe Arnold toll-gate, possibly embellished by the artist to represent a more romantic scene than it actually was. It was the site of the gruesome murder of Edward Woodcock and his grandson on 18 June 1856.

Woodcocks Cottage, Thorpe Arnold, 1998. Still standing very close to the modern highway, it is remarkable that the building has not suffered the fate of so many toll-keepers' cottages which have been demolished in modern road widening schemes.

Woodcut of William Brown, alias Peppermint Billy, published on Saturday 26 July 1856, the day after his execution in Leicester and printed in a broadsheet published by T. Warwick, 5 Union Street, Leicester.

William Brown, a native of Scalford, the next village north-west of Thorpe Arnold, was nicknamed Peppermint Billy because of his liking for strong peppermints. He came from a notorious family: his father had a criminal record and two brothers were sentenced to transportation for theft.

In 1843 he appeared before the Leicestershire Quarter Sessions for stealing a set of silver spoons at Newtown Linford. At the trial he said he was framed so that his accuser could take his girlfriend, and that the spoons had been given to him by his mother. He also had a previous criminal record and for this latest crime he was sentenced to ten years' transportation to Van Diemen's Land (Tasmania). He returned to London in 1856. He must have worked hard during ten years on the island to save sufficient capital to pay for his passage back to England but he returned an embittered man, who was heard to say on the journey home that he intended killing the man who had caused him to be deported.

Brown returned to Leicestershire as a convict on licence and was treated with great suspicion by his fellow villagers and the people of Melton Mowbray. When Edward Woodcock and his grandson were murdered he was the immediate suspect; at his trial at the Leicestershire Assize Court damning statements were submitted.

Edward Woodcock was the collector of tolls at the toll-gate below Thorpe Arnold Hill and lived in a small cottage near the gate; his grandson James Woodcock aged ten lived with him, sleeping in the same bed. It was Edward's duty to unlock the gate and collect the tolls day and night. It was presumed that Brown approached the cottage at around midnight on 18 June and shouted 'Gate' in the traditional way of travellers who wished to pass along the road at night-time. The gatekeeper got up, put on his coat and opened the door, whereupon the murderer produced a pistol and shot him, the ball passing through his coat and into his body. The shot was not fatal.

Even though Edward Woodcock was an elderly man, he was fit and healthy and he tackled Brown, who dropped the pistol where it was later found, producing a knife from his pocket at the same time as a tobacco-stopper of a strange design that fell to the floor and was later identified as belonging to him. Edward put up a valiant fight even though he had been shot through the chest but he eventually succumbed to twelve stab wounds.

James was woken by the noise and it is thought came to his grandad's assistance. Brown stabbed him in the abdomen and slit his throat, nearly severing his head from his body.

Brown's motive was robbery; he had visited the toll-gate house the day before to spy out the lay of the land and had a confrontation with the gatekeeper according to Henry Reed, who was working with Brown cleaning out a ditch nearby.

The bodies of Edward Woodcock and his grandson were discovered by Alfred Routen, a baker from Asfordby, who was transporting bread in his carrier's cart to Grantham. Stopping at the Thorpe Arnold toll-gate at 4.20 a.m. on 19 June he shouted 'Gate'. No one answered so he entered the cottage and discovered the two mutilated bodies.

He ran up Thorpe Hill to the first house in the village and woke William Bishop, shouting 'The poor old toll-bar man lies dead'. They woke up the village constable, John Clayton. Thomas Barwis, a surgeon from Melton Mowbray, was called and had the bodies removed; he conducted a post mortem the following day. Frederick Goodyer was appointed detective on the case, which attracted national publicity.

Principally as a result of statements obtained from James Birbridge (Thorpe Arnold), Henry Reed (Melton Mowbray), William Moore (Melton Mowbray), Francis O'Hare (Melton Mowbray), Thomas Roberts (Constable from Scalford), and William Fox (Scalford), Brown was apprehended at Wetherby in Yorkshire. William Eccles, the parish constable, had read an account of the murder and a description of the suspect published in the *Leeds Mercury*. Frederick Goodyer and Constable Edward Bishop travelled north and brought the prisoner back for trial. The trial opened at the Midsummer Assizes on 14 July 1856. The evidence was overwhelming and Peppermint Billy was sentenced to hang by Judge Jervis.

A scaffold was erected in front of Welford Road jail. Billy was given his last breakfast at 6 a.m. and with the County Sheriff in attendance he was escorted on to the platform. The Chaplain read the first part of the burial service, the bolt was drawn and at 8 a.m. on 25 July 1856 Peppermint Billy was launched into eternity at the end of the hangman's rope in front of many thousands of cheering Leicester citizens. This was the last public hanging in England.

Verse printed on Warwick's broadsheet of July 1856

You feeling Christians pay attention, young and old of each degree,
While unto you I now will mention, a sad and awful tragedy;
Two unoffending fellow creatures have been murdered you shall hear,
Edward Woodcock & his grandson, near Melton Mowbray, Leicestershire.

CHORUS
Think, oh, think of Edward Woodcock, and his little grandson dear,
Basely murder'd and mutilated, near Melton Mowbray, Leicestershire.

Twas at the toll-gate near Thorpe Arnold, this old man did used to dwell,
He was upright in all his dealings, and was respected very well;
With his grandson he lived happy, and the truth I tell to you;
But now, alas! He has been murder'd, at the age of seventy-two.

At four o'clock on Thursday morning, on the eighteenth day of June,
A baker went to pay the tollgate – saw poor Woodcock's awful doom;
Streams of crimson blood were flowing – what a shocking sight to see!
His feeble age did not protect him, from a murderer's cruelty.

His innocent and loving grandchild, a little boy of ten years old;
Oh! when they saw his bleeding body, the fearful truth was plainly told,
That in the silent hour of night, when all around was cloth'd in gloom,
The murderer struck the fatal blows, that sent them to the silent tomb.

Edward Woodcock and his grandson in the churchyard now do lay,
Their troubles in this world of strife, for ever now have pass'd away;
The grass will grow around their bed, and the weeping willows wave,
To mark the spot where these victims do rest within silent the grave.

Crude wood engraving printed on the Warwick broadsheet. Cuts such as this were repeatedly used to illustrate grief. This had possibly been used on more than one broadsheet sold in the streets of Leicester.

BURTON LAZARS

Church of St James, Burton Lazars, 1791. This engraving of a drawing by J. Pridden shows the striking monument to William Squires erected to the left of the church in 1780.

Burton Lazars Hall, the home of George Coats JP, 1905.

Spectators standing in the main stand at the Melton Hunt Steeplechase held on Burton Flats south of Burton Lazars, 1 April 1908. On race day a continuous procession of people made their way down Burton Street, Melton Mowbray, on their way to the racecourse.

Cartoon by Snaffles drawn entitled 'Race course jottings', 1913. It shows Major Hughes Onslow winning the main race at the Melton Hunt Steeplechase at Burton Flats.

The Prince of Wales jumping one of the fences in a steeplechase on Burton Flats, late 1920s. At this time during the fox-hunting season he lived at Craven Lodge on Burton Road, Melton Mowbray (*see The Melton Mowbray Album*, pp. 90 and 91). On the death of his father George V in 1935, he became King Edward VIII. He reigned for 325 days but was never crowned because he had publicly announced that he was to marry Mrs Wallis Simpson, an American citizen who embarked on her second divorce in 1935. This marriage was bitterly opposed by the Archbishop of Canterbury and the British Prime Minister Stanley Baldwin. If the Prince of Wales had not indulged in sporting activities in and around Melton Mowbray he would probably not have met Mrs Simpson at Burrough Court (below), only a few miles away to the south of Burton Lazars. It was a meeting that eventually changed the course of English history.

Burrough Court, 1904.

BRENTINGBY

Engraving of a drawing by J. Pridden of Brentingby Chapel, which was dedicated to the Blessed Virgin Mary, 1791. This religious building became redundant in the 1950s and was purchased for conversion into a private house in 1978. From archaeological evidence obtained prior to conversion, it would seem that the original building could have been laid out some time around the year 1150. Saxon/Norman pottery was uncovered and evidence exists that many changes were made to the original building over the centuries, including a reduction in size in 1660.

The Manor House, Brentingby 1791. It was built by the Hartopp family in the 1650s.

Brentingby Gate House in the 1930s, a narrow cottage built at the side of the railway track in the 1860s on the minimum of land. The whole structure vibrated when the steam-driven express thundered by, day and night. This gatehouse serviced a field road used by the local farming community when their lands were divided on the construction of the Peterborough to Nottingham railway line in the 1840s.

Haize (left) and Fred being shod by Malcolm Kelham, farrier, at Brentingby Lodge Farm, 1977. Ian Manchester is holding the reigns to Haize, with Hemming Franz holding Fred's reins. Geoff Pyzer is preparing a horseshoe for the first fitting.

WYFORDBY

Main Street, Wyfordby, with the church of St Mary on the left, 1793. The church was built in the thirteenth century but fell into disrepair and underwent extensive restoration in 1869. In the centre of the engraving are two thatched and possibly mud-walled cottages; on the left is a stone-built manorial dovecote.

The remains of lock number seven on the Melton Mowbray to Oakham Canal at Wyfordby, 1967. The photographer stood below the step looking up into the lock. The gates, stone quoins and bricks were removed over a hundred years before this photograph was taken. Today, even what remained in 1967 has been removed in a land drainage programme.

FREEBY

The early fourteenth-century church of St Mary shown in an engraving from a drawing by J. Pridden published in 1792.

Main Street, Freeby, during the First World War. This view has changed little during the last 100 years. In the centre at the bottom of the road is the small Congregational chapel; founded in 1665, it was one of the first in the country.

Harvest time at Freeby, cutting wheat with a tractor and binder, 1946. Left to right: Walter Giffin checking the binder twine dispenser assisted by Claude Manchester with Ian Manchester at the controls. The same three people are shown below on a stationary binder and Fordson tractor.

Frank Wright (left) and Stephen Manchester, muck carting at Freeby, 1946.

Nancy Manchester with son Ian on a Standard Fordson tractor, 1943.

SAXBY

Saxby church prior to 1788, the year when it was demolished on the instruction of the 4th Lord Harborough of Stapleford Hall.

St Peter's church, Saxby, 1794. It was constructed in 1789 on the site of the first church.

Saxby church in 1904 when its Vicar was the Rural Dean and JP, the Revd Peter Freeland Gorst MA.

Decorative spire on St Peter's church.

The spire and tower being repaired in the 1930s. The five photographs on these two pages mark important times in the history of St Peter's, Saxby. On the instructions of Lord Harborough, the famous eighteenth-century architect John Richardson was commissioned to design a new church in the 1780s. He based his design on the London churches created by Nicholas Hawksmoor. The main feature is the square west tower, which is topped by an octagonal spire with two tiers of lucarnes or small windows (see photograph top right).

Square-headed and cruciform Saxon brooches, beads and tweezers discovered at Saxby in the 1890/1 excavations for the Bourne railway track.

Cinerary urns uncovered from a large burial site during the same excavations. During the Saxon period the river valley from Saxby to Garthorpe was a major site of occupation, a fact which has been confirmed by archaeological remains uncovered in recent years. Romano-British and Saxon remains intermingle, covering a considerable and virtually unbroken time sequence up until the Norman Conquest in 1066. Saxby was possibly the main centre of population in the area and a stronghold for the period 400–600 AD, the time span covered when an accurate analysis was done of recovered pagan inhumations. With the spread of Christianity throughout the country, village churches were built and settlements developed around them. The large Saxon tribal gathering was possibly dispersed throughout the neighbouring valleys.

Waiting-room at Saxby station, 1967. A waiting-room was first built and came into operation in 1849, only to be demolished when the track was realigned in the 1890s. This building was opened in August 1892 and closed on 6 February 1961.

Porters at Saxby station, c. 1930. Edward Mitchel (left) was from London and lodged in the village of Saxby. Frederick Pickaver (right) lived at the Wyfordby railway crossing gatehouse. In the background stands a Johnson/Deeley 0-6-0 3F built in around 1885; it was ex-Midland Railway with rebuilt Belpaire boilers.

Saxby junction in the 1950s showing the branch line leading to Wymondham and on to Bourne with the main London line on the right. It was in this area that the Saxon finds shown opposite were discovered.

SAXBY MAY DAY SONG

Re-member us for May is here, And thus we do be-gin —— To lead our lives in righteousness Un-less we die in sin. —— We have been ramb-ling all the night And almost all the day. —— And now return-ing back a-gain, We have brought you a branch of May. ——

A branch of may we have brought you,
    And at your door it stands.
It is but a sprout but it's well budded-out
    By the work of our Lord's hands.

The hedges and trees they are so green,
    As green as any leaf.
Our Heavenly Father waters them
    With His heavenly dew so sweet.

The life of man it is but a span,
    It flutters like a flower.
We're here to-day and gone tomorrow,
    And we are dead in an hour.

The moon shines bright and the stars give light,
    For nations seem so gay.
So God bless you all, both great and small,
    And send you a joyous May.

These verses and the tune to the Saxby May Day song were passed down from generation to generation of Saxby residents. Fanny Skerritt, who lived in the thatched cottage (below) that stood off the Garthorpe Road, sang this song when the village children escorted the May Queen with her garland around the village and also at the maypole, as did the author's mother-in-law Alice Mason, née Smith, on May Day before the First World War (see also *The Melton Mowbray Album*, p. 94).

May Day celebrations no longer take place in Saxby but they are still an annual event in the nearby village of Wymondham. Above, Wymondham and Saxby children are dancing around the maypole on Wymondham village green, 1990s.

Mrs Lucy Spur of Saxby, 1927. A Saxby stalwart, she encouraged village traditions between the two world wars.

An express from Leicester en route to the east coast via Bourne. Double-headed with a Hughes Fowler 5–MT and a Midland compound 4 P, passing a line of wooden ironstone wagons at Wymondham Junction, to the east of Saxby station, 1946 – two years before nationalization.

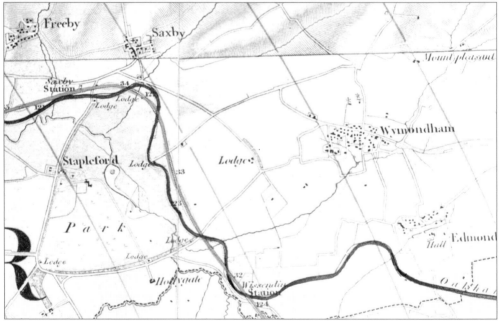

Section of the 1835 edition of the Ordnance Survey map, revised in 1867. On this map Stapleford Park is clearly defined; the Melton Mowbray to Oakham Canal and the Nottingham to Peterborough railway track are intertwined. When the map was first drawn in 1835 the railway did not exist. Most of the 'Battles of Saxby' took place between the village of Saxby and Stapleford to the north-east of the lake in Stapleford Park, and are briefly described on page 67.

BATTLES OF SAXBY

Some of the great stories that were told over many glasses of strong ale in the local taverns before the First World War were accounts of the 'Battles of Saxby', embellished by many who took part!

The 6th Earl of Harborough, a shareholder in the Melton Mowbray to Oakham Canal, took exception to the building of the Nottingham to Peterborough railway line over his land, especially through the enclosed park. This quarrelsome lord had given notice that 'Surveyors will not be permitted to enter upon his lordship's land', but on Tuesday 12 November 1843 surveyors did just that! In a resolution passed at a meeting of the canal company in April 1843 support was given to Lord Harborough and, backed by this statement, the lord's gamekeeper John Todd stopped the railway surveyors from entering the land along the tow-path. A surveyor drew a pistol and Todd shouted 'Fire away.' He was backed by a large number of farm and canal workers.

A general fracas took place, nine railway surveyors were captured and put in a cart to convey them to the nearest JP; one could not be found so they were unceremoniously tipped on the ground to be charged with trespass the next day at the Melton Mowbray police court.

On 14 November battle recommenced. The railway surveyors arrived with three prize fighters from Nottingham and a large contingent of navvies. Lord Harborough's steward, Fabling, had around forty men in support when the two sides met on Saxby Bridge. Both sets of men were armed with shillelaghs. Before battle could commence five county policemen arrived and threatened to arrest the first person who committed an assault.

But the day could not pass without some confrontation so it was decided that a trial of strength would take place; both parties crossed arms and began a pushing match. The contestants tried to force each other over the parapet of the bridge much to the amusement of the numerous spectators. A truce was called, but then a railway surveyor laid out a measuring chain and this was seized and broken in the ensuing scuffle.

A truce was finally agreed until the results of the survey could be heard. The railway workers disregarded this and on 16 November returned to the attack with over 100 men, entering the park from Saxby Bridge and climbing over the deer fence palings off the Wymondham road. They began measuring the land until they came opposite the cottage near the lake (see engraving on p. 81). Lord Harborough was enraged and ordered Fabling to attack the intruders. Fabling ordered the measuring chains to be broken up; this was resisted. Brown, the lock-keeper at Saxby, rendered great assistance, sending railway workers head over heels with every blow. The railway workers used their measuring poles as lances and charged the defenders of the park. Barricades of wagons and hurdles were erected on Fabling's instructions and a fire-engine was used to pump water on to the enemy. The railway workers lost heart and retreated when Lord Harborough arrived with two cannon, which he had removed from his yacht on the lake and strapped to a cart. How powerful these cannon were is not known but the sight of them was enough to make the surveyors and navvies retreat. The railway 'army' had white ribbons in their buttonholes to distinguish them from Lord Harborough's troops, who were each paid 2s 6d per day.

A number of summonses were issued and John Todd, the gamekeeper, was charged with assault. On 26 March 1845 three cases were tried at Leicester Assizes and Chief Justice Tindal found ten of the railway workers guilty of assault and shown guilty of causing a riot on Lord Harborough's land; he imprisoned them for one month and each was fined 1s.

There were two further encounters on the 24 and 28 November 1845. On the 24th Lord Harborough charged the railway workers in a light carriage and, capturing one of the railway surveyors' chaises, he ordering the wheels to be sawn off. On the 28th he actually entered into a bout of fisticuffs with one of the railway solicitors. About 300 men were involved in each of these encounters and a number of court cases resulted. Lord Harborough was found not guilty on all charges!

The railway did not enter Stapleford Park during the lifetime of the 6th and last Lord Harborough. An attempt was made to pass the park to the south but this failed because a projected tunnel was not excavated correctly. The Nottingham to Peterborough railway line was laid along the northern boundary of the park, and this resulted in the infamous Lord Harborough curve that passed over a wooden bridge and was a curse to all engine-drivers using the track. The trains had to slow down, causing much annoyance to the fireman and driver who had to maintain a head of steam in difficult circumstances.

Remains of the four-arched culverts that carried the Melton Mowbray to Oakham Canal over the stream that runs from Garthorpe through Saxby to the River Eye in Stapleford Park, 1967. This was the scene of most of the Battles of Saxby.

The Melton Mowbray to Oakham Canal at Saxby, 1967. In the background stand the remains of the pile bridge: on the left-hand embankment, near the telegraph pole, can be seen two blackened stumps, all that remained of the main supporting piles that held up the wooden bridge built on Lord Harborough's curve. This deviation from the projected line caused great inconvenience to the railway company; it was the result of Lord Harborough's obstinacy and can be clearly seen on the map reproduced on page 66. The track was eventually straightened, long after his death.

STAPLEFORD

Stapleford Park with church and hall in the background, 1790. The hall is built in a mixture of styles ranging from those of about 1500 to the turn of the twentieth century. The Tudor wing was partly rebuilt in 1633 by Inigo Jones; its walls contain many interesting paintings of religious and secular subjects. The north front is late seventeenth century and is an excellent example of architecture of the reign of Charles II. In 1775 Capability Brown was paid £31 10s 0d to advise on the laying out of the park; it is doubtful if he produced a complete plan for the alterations.

Hall and lake, 1990s. In 1402 Robert Sherrard purchased the park from the Earl of Lancaster. It remained in the Sherrard family until the death of the 6th and last Lord Harborough in 1859. Lady Harborough née Eliza Temple retained the hall and estate until it was sold in 1885 to James Hornsby. In 1894 it was bought by John Gretton and remained in the Gretton family until it was purchased in 1986 by Bob Paynton, who converted it into a hotel. When Bob died in 1996 his wife Wendy sold it to the present owner, Peter de Savary.

The old wing at Stapleford Hall restored on the instruction of Lady Abigail Sherrard, *c.* 1905. The façade includes twelve niches which contain unique carved figures, many erected in the fifteenth century.

St Mary Magdalene church, Stapleford, 1795. Built by Christopher Staveley of Melton Mowbray, the church was designed by the famous London architect George Richardson who exhibited his plans for it at the Royal Academy in 1783. It is doubtful whether this church was built on the site of the previous building, demolished on the instructions of the 4th Earl of Harborough. In the seventeenth century Stapleford deer park was created after the village was cleared. The village had been granted a weekly market by the King in 1308.

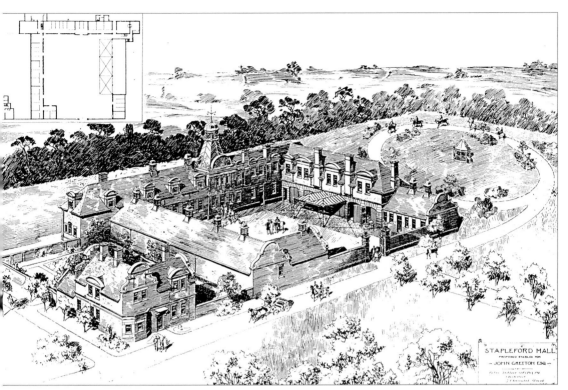

Plan and drawing for the proposed stables at Stapleford Park by Peter Dollar, commissioned by John Gretton in 1899. A modified version was eventually built without the fine house to the left of the main block.

Stapleford Park stables, *c.* 1905. This is considered to be the finest stable block in the fox-hunting country centred on Melton Mowbray.

Detail from a painting by Marcus Gheeraerts the younger (c. 1561–1635) of Abigail Lady Sherrard. It was through her inspiration that Stapleford Hall was rebuilt and extended in the 1630s.

Detail from a painting by Marcus Gheeraerts the younger of William, 1st Lord Sherrard, at the age of thirty-four. He was knighted by James I in 1622 and made a Baron by King Charles I in 1627. William was born in 1588; in 1620 he married Abigail (left), eldest daughter of Cecil Cave of Stamford Hall, Leicestershire.

Peter de Savary, Chairman of Stapleford Park, an outpost of the Carnegie Club. The 1st Lord Sherrard and his wife Abigail laid the foundations of a unique building. Peter de Savary is following in their footsteps, maintaining an exceptionally fine English country house in a twentieth-century setting.

During the Gretton occupancy this was the ante-room, seen here in the 1950s. It is now the reception area for this famous country house hotel.

Long gallery, 1950s. The restoration and alteration of this part of the hall was started by John Gretton; ambitious plans were made to convert this to a magnificent ballroom but the work was never completed. Lack of funds ensured that the decorations were never finished and uncoated cement rendering covered the walls with a plain plastered ceiling for decades. Cottesmore Hunt balls and many fund-raising whist drives were nevertheless held there. Bob Payton converted this gallery into bedroom suites.

The three children of Colonel John Gretton MP at the entrance to the hall, 1930s. John in the centre succeeded as owner when his father died in 1947. Julie is on the left and Bridgit on the right.

George Leaf, joint huntsman to the Quorn hounds (with Tom Bishop) for the seasons 1905/06 to 1917/18, and the Prince of Wales, later King Edward VIII, at Stapleford Park, c. 1914.

Colonel John Gretton at one of the many meets of the Cottesmore Hounds at Stapleford Park, 1910.

The Market Cross, Stapleford, *c.* 1930. This was the site of the weekly market granted by Edward II (1307–27). This cross was possibly restored by the 4th Earl of Harborough after he rebuilt the church in the eighteenth century. On the engraving printed at the top of page 69, the base of the cross is shown to the right of the hall near a ruined arch left over from the first church, which was of Saxon origin. In 1089 Henry de Ferrers granted the church to the monks of Tutbury Priory in Staffordshire.

The removal of the village of Stapleford probably began in around 1500 as a land clearance to make a deer park and continued under successive owners. To the north of the Market Cross house platforms are clearly defined in the grassland. The village would have extended into what is now woodland adjacent to the cross; this photograph, taken in 1914, shows a few of the cottages that survived standing in the woods. They were demolished in the same year.

An early thatched cottage with Stapleford school, *c.* 1914. The cottage was demolished in 1914 and the school was pulled down in 1970.

A number of thatched cottages which were part of the original village of Stapleford were demolished in 1914. John Gretton built this row of fine cottages, photographed in 1920, to replace those that had been destroyed a few years earlier. They still stand in the trees off the main driveway to Stapleford Park.

During the First and Second World Wars Stapleford Hall was used as a convalescent home by the Leicestershire Red Cross for wounded soldiers. The two photographs on this page were taken at approximately the same time in 1942. Left to right, standing: Chauffeur Mr MacDonald, -?-, Peggy Ladkin, Beryl Jeffries. Seated: ? Pollard, Stanya ?.

Stapleford Park Convalescent Home, November 1942. Left to right, back row: Beryl Jeffries, Mrs Johnson, Cook at hall, -?-, Sergeant Olive, -?-, -?-, -?-, -?-. Middle row: -?-, Nurse Hart, Matron, Lady Floyd (Lord Gretton's sister), Lady Lansborough, Sister Morris, Stanya ?. Front row: -?-, Rt Hon. Julie Gretton, Rt Hon. Bridgit Floyd Gretton, Peggy Ladkin.

Owing to the shortage of manpower during the Second World War the Land Army was formed, recruiting young girls to work on the farms of Great Britain. Stapleford estate took part in this scheme. In this photograph, possibly taken in the walled garden during 1943, are the eight girls who worked in the hall grounds and on the Stapleford farms. Back row, left to right: Lil Bishop, Mavis ?, Pauline ?, Helen ?, -?-. Front row: Joan Austin, Joan ?, Bettine Birch.

Holygate Farm, the key farm on the Stapleford estate, 1990s. It was to a farm in this locality that Joseph Hickman moved to take up the tenancy in the late eighteenth century. He worked the land for the 4th Earl of Harborough and a low-lying hill to the south of the farm is still called Hickman's Hill. The author of this book is directly descended from this farmer, six generations removed.

The Stapleford Park lion reserve opened at Easter 1968. It was a joint venture between Lord Gretton and Dick Chipperfield who owned a lion reserve in Natal, South Africa. Philip Maxwell and his wife ran a small zoo adjacent to the reserve. This photograph shows Zulu, one of the dominant male lions of the Stapleford pride. Visitors drove around the reserve in their cars passing close to the well-fed lions, whose night-time roars could be heard for miles around – a strange sound in the stillness of late evening in the East Midlands.

Miniature railway, 1995. One of the main features of Stapleford Park when the hall and grounds were open to the public after the Second World War was the miniature railway. The first section ran from the stables to the station near the hall and was opened by the Earl of Northesk on 18 May 1958. Over the years some lines were closed and others extended. The track still runs down past the lake and on certain days it is open to the public.

Lady Nutting of Quenby Hall leaving the stewards' marquee with the Duchess of Gloucester, Leicestershire County Show, 1951. Over the centuries many events have taken place in Stapleford Park. For a few years the Leicestershire County Show was held on the land between the hall and the lake, a magnificent setting.

Stapleford Country Festival, 28 August 1995. In recent years a festival has been run in the park over August Bank Holiday weekend. The main attraction is the Steam Fair. This is a charitable event organized by Lady Jennifer Gretton on behalf of LOROS (Leicestershire Organisation for the Relief of Suffering). Left to right: Sharon Grech with Georgina Grech in the pushchair, Amy Grech, Chloe Grech, Angela Edwards with Harriett Edwards in the pushchair.

Lord Harborough's cottage, Stapleford Park, 1832. This cottage was built by Philip, Earl of Harborough, for his mistress, the Drury Lane actress Emma Sarah Love. Lord Harborough entertained his mistress in this cottage for over twenty-five years. They met when he was a single man; Emma Love had entered into marriage with a Mr Granby Calcroft who would not divorce her. She was not accepted by Leicestershire society. When Lord Harborough married Eliza Temple of Stowe he maintained his wife in the hall and his mistress in his cottage, in the Cottage Plantation. He built extensive water gardens so that he and his mistress could spend idyllic hours in a punt in front of the beautiful cottage. Lord Harborough died in 1859. His widow pulled down the cottage and rebuilt a smaller version with most of the usable stone at nearby Whissendine on land that was part of her estate, so providing a home for Emma Love.

The larder used to hang venison, 1880s. The larder also appears in the engraving above. It was constructed over an extensive vault used to store wine and cheeses.

The chimney in the Cottage Plantation, 1998. This is all that is left of the beautiful cottage illustrated at the top of page 81. Until a few years ago the enormous chimney breast was used by forestry workers as their bothy. The author has fond memories of sitting there next to the large fire, eating sandwiches and drinking hot tea with estate workers in the late 1940s.

Remains of the sluice gates and the watercourse that was built to transfer river water to the pond and water gardens which were laid out in the trees in front of the cottage for the pleasure of the 6th and last Lord Harborough and his mistress.

Harborough Cottage, Stapleford Road, Whissendine, 1925. The cottage was built by Lord Harborough's widow for Emma Sarah Love in the 1860s but she did not live in it for many years, preferring to retire to Brighton, far away from Leicestershire high society which had rejected her.

WYMONDHAM

Wymondham Grammar School, 1903. Sir John Sedley, who died in 1638, left the sum of £400 to the village. As a result of this, a charitable trust was formed for the education of the children of Wymondham. Considerable farmland was purchased in Melton Mowbray to provide an income from the rents. In 1877 the trust sold just over 6 acres of land to enable the Great Northern and North Western Railway companies to build the Northern station at Melton Mowbray for £6,321 13s 6d. From this income Wymondham Grammar School was built. It was opened on 27 September 1882. After educational reforms it closed its doors in 1906. It is now a private house and design studio.

The remains of the early seventeenth-century dovecote that is now part of the Old Rectory. After the church, it is possibly the oldest stone structure in the village.

A solid silver cup presented in 1935 as a replica of the original trophy which was donated to the Wymondham and District Horticultural Society by Sir Lindsey Everard MP in 1928 and is now in the hands of the Parish Council; Sir Lindsey also donated the replica. The Horticultural Society was formed in around 1893. Its annual show took place on what is now the Sir John Sedley Recreational field; the last was held in 1939.

At a parish meeting called on 19 December 1919 it was decided to form a brass band in the village. This picture was taken at the annual flower show on the showground and is possibly the first photograph of the band. Back row, left to right: -?-, William Hickman, Randle Pollard, Jack Pollard, Fred Meadows, Bill Golling, -?-, -?-, Don Alexander. Front row: Jack Whiles, Bill Welbourne, Jack Welbourne, Jack Pollard, Archie Alexander, George Pickaver, Jack Whiles, Ted Fawkes, Jimmy Tysoe.

Wymondham Brass Band, *c.* 1930. Left to right: Fred Meadows, Jack Pollard jnr, William Welbourne, Jack Whiles, 'Dick' Whiles, John Pulford, Randall Pollard, Jack Welbourne, Cecil Hickman, Frank Pollard, Bill Naylor, Fred Berry.

Arthur Johnson's grocer's, Main Street, Wymondham, 1960s. The shop was run by Gordon Tandy and behind the counter is John ('Friday') Whiles, with Ted Huddlestone offering advice.

John Morris's antique shop, Chapel Lane, 1970. Built by Edward Garnham in the 1880s, this was originally a hosiery factory, reaching peak production during the First World War when it produced knitted socks for the troops in the Flanders trenches. Later for many years it was a grocer's and general store run by Miss May Gill.

Cottesmore Hunt, Wymondham Village Green, *c.* 1930. Note William Lambert's bakery (centre background) with the loft door above the window where sacks of flour were raised by a hoist from the pavement below. This building is now the premises of Old Bakery Antiques.

Alec Fiford, Raymond Sykes and Cliff Fiford standing in Pudding Bag Lane (now Bursnalls Lane), 1936. In the background is the harness and tack room to Sycamore House, the home of the Hon Captain Mountjoy Fane. Most of the building was demolished in the 1950s when Sycamore House was developed into four houses.

The Oakham Canal in Wymondham Roughs, 1990s. This tranquil stretch of water is maintained by the Leicestershire Trust for Nature Conservation.

Wymondham mile-post, Stapleford Park, 1970. This post was used as a bollard for tying up barges in the parish of Wymondham. It was on the north bank of the Oakham Canal near the present Wymondham Gatehouse on the Melton Mowbray to Peterborough railway line, Glebe Road.

George Bursnall's shop, Main Street, Wymondham, c. 1905. It stood in front of what is now Laburnum Cottage. George, a boot and shoemaker, later moved his business to Pudding Bag Lane which was renamed Bursnalls Lane by the Borough Council in the 1980s.

Entrance to Church Lane in front of The Bowery, Wymondham, *c.* 1890. Holding the horse is Arthur Johnson (grocer and draper), son of Richard Johnson of Garthorpe (shoemaker) and Elizabeth Talton. Arthur Johnson was married to Mary Jane Cooper; they emigrated to Canada where they both died.

Wymondham Church of England School, Main Street, Wymondham, 1909. Back row, left to right: Mr Dyke (schoolmaster), the three Getliffe boys, -?-, -?-, -?-, -?-, -?-, Neil Finlay, Miss Bird, Miss Cissy Huddlestone. Third row: Harold Coulston, Jack Whiles, -?-, Kate Whiles, Dolly Bursnall, -?-, Gladys Hickman, -?-, -?-. Second row: -?-, -?-, Hilda Hickman, -?-, -?-, ? Hickman, -?-, Mona Barfoot, -?-. Front row: -?-, Florrie Whiles, -?-, -?-, Geoff Bursnall, -?-.

Celebrations for the Silver Jubilee of King George V, 1935. Front row, left to right: Mrs Willet, Mrs Golling, Mrs Ada Blechschmidt, E. Fawkes, H. Bottom, Sid Hickman. Second row: Tom Pickaver, Captain Mountjoy Fane, Dick Whiles, Norman Whitaker, Harry Weston. Charlie Freeman is raising his glass to the King and Queen in the background. A happy band of revellers walked around the village toasting the King and Queen; in this photograph they are outside Thorne Cottage on the Main Street.

Planting an oak on Wymondham Village Green to mark the Silver Jubilee of King George V, 1935. Left to right, tree planters: Mr C. Harvey, Victor Grenfell, Hon Mrs Mountjoy Fane. Girl Guides: -?-, Muriel Whiles, Jessie Sykes, Margery Sykes, Brenda Fawkes. Spectators: Harry Weston, -?-, Nancy Bartram, Mrs Perrin, -?-, Ada Blechschmidt. The tree was destroyed by vandals during the Second World War!

Louisa Tysoe standing outside her cottage, which is now part of 21 Sycamore Lane, 1917. Born in 1862, she died in May 1963. A special peal of bells was rung in September 1962 to celebrate her 100th birthday.

Sarah Elizabeth Whiles with her daughter Lucy Beryl, standing outside Sims Cottage, Sycamore Lane, 1917. Sarah was born in 1879. She married Harry Fiford. Known as 'Granny Fiford' for many years, she died in 1981 at the age of 103.

John Whiles while in the flying corps during the First World War. He lived at Barley Mow Cottage, which was on Sycamore Lane and was named after the public house run at the same premises by John Large in the 1850s.

Alexander 'Jock' Miller with his wife Lottie and son Charlie, 1930. Jock was the village postman for very many years. Charlie was killed in a motorcycle accident in 1932. Millers Cottage on Main Street is named after this family.

Tapestry stitched by Charlotte Elizabeth Day, daughter of William Day, *c.* 1840. It shows her home, Wymondham House, and the church of St Peter.

The Grenfell boys, Harold, Cecil and Victor, 1940. All three had interesting naval careers. This photograph was taken outside their home The Rookery where they stayed with their mother and father, Colonel J.R. Grenfell, when they were on leave.

The north side of Main Street, Wymondham, 1905. The two shops with the crenellations are Arthur Johnsons's grocer's and George William Bursnall's shoemaker's. Also shown are the steps leading to the loft above Benjamin Jackson Ashwell's bakehouse.

The Ranters chapel, Sycamore Lane, 1965. The chapel was built in 1826 for the Primitive Methodists who were given the name 'Ranters' because they paraded through the streets, loudly proclaiming their faith. The photograph was taken from the Rectory drive. This unique little chapel was demolished in 1965.

Choir of St Peter's church, 1906. The organist is William Dyke, schoolmaster, and on the extreme right is the Vicar, Revd William Hill Lee MA; sitting next to him is Mr Willet.

Unveiling of the War Memorial in Wymondham churchyard by Colonel John Gretton of Stapleford Park, 1 November 1919.

Wymondham Rovers FC, 1979/80. Centre background: Bruce Roberts, manager. Back row, left to right: Paul Bettinson, Chris Roberts, Neil Medhurst, John Collins, John Ward, Simon Naylor, Gary Holsworth. Front row: Danny Malony, Jeremy Hancock, Tim Hickman (captain), Ian Hickman, Colin Connelly, Jason Howden.

Hunters Arms Hotel, Edmondthorpe Road, Wymondham. This is the birthplace of the cheese we now call Stilton. It was built as a farmhouse and was the home of Francis Pawlett for over forty years during the eighteenth century; she developed the modern Stilton cheese. For further information consult *The History of Stilton Cheese*. In 1997 this building ceased to be a public house.

Edmondthorpe and Wymondham station, *c.* 1936. The photographer stood underneath Butt Lane bridge. This station opened on 1 May 1894 and closed to passenger traffic on 2 March 1959.

Edmondthorpe and Wymondham railway station looking east, July 1961.

Edmondthorpe and Wymondham station, Monday morning 29 December 1958. This photograph was taken from the Nottingham to Spalding train as it departed east for the next stop at South Witham. The porter/signalman, Fred Heal, is just returning to the signal box.

Edmondthorpe and Wymondham station goods yard, looking west from the Butt Lane bridge, July 1961. The disused cattle pens and the engine shed are to the left.

THISTLETON GAP

On the left stands a belt of trees known as Thistleton Gap. It was in a field across Fosse Lane, to the north-west and in a natural hollow, that in 1811 the first defence of the heavyweight championship of the world took place – a bare fist fight between the champion of the world, Tom Cribb of England, and the American challenger, Tom Molyneux.

Tom Cribb was proclaimed the champion of England when he beat Jem Belcher on 1 February 1809. Cribb fought his first public fight at Highgate on 7 January 1805 against George Maddox. The fight lasted seventy-six rounds and went on for two hours and ten minutes until Maddox could not take any more punishment. A round lasted for as long as the contestants could defend themselves. When a fighter was knocked down or winded he was allowed to rest for thirty seconds; if he did not rise to restart the fight, his opponent was declared the winner. Cribb first fought the American Molyneux at Copthal Common on 1 December 1810, in a controversial fight where Cribb was declared the winner and world champion.

On 28 September 1811 Tom Cribb and Tom Molyneux fought on a wooden stage in a stubble field near the copse of trees known as Thistleton Gap in the parish of Wymondham. Various estimates have been made on the number of spectators present, ranging from 10,000 to 20,000; if the lower figure is accepted it is still an incredible amount of people. The nobility and aristocracy were represented by Lord Berkeley Craven, Major Mellish, Captain Barclay, Sir Francis Boynton, General Grosvenor, Sir Henry Smith, The Marquis of Queensberry, Lord Pomfret and Sir Charles Aston, the Prince Regent's agent. The country's honour was at stake; the thought of a negro being declared the champion of England and the world was totally abhorrent to the nobility of the time. After the Copthal Common fight, where Cribb's seconds had been accused of cheating by a ruse which extended the resting period well over thirty seconds, the sporting fraternity was worried that Cribb could be beaten. Captain Barclay put Cribb through a course of extensive training and raised him to the peak of fitness. Molyneux, on the other hand, succumbed to the good life, eating too many steaks and drinking too much red wine. On 29 January 1811 at the Fives Court in Leicester Square, London, Cribb accepted Molyneux's challenge to fight for the championship of the world. A site off the Great North Road was fixed. The arrangements were made, the venue a stubble field just in the parish of Wymondham. Tom Cribb rented rooms at the Black Bull Inn on Witham Common, a famous coaching inn on the Great North Road and 5 miles north of The New Inn at Greetham where Tom Molyneux was staying. 'Gentleman' John Jackson, an ex-prize-fighter was appointed referee. Cribb's seconds were John Gulley and Joe Ward; Molyneux's were Bill Richmond and Bill Gibbons. The fight began at 12.20 p.m. and lasted for eleven rounds over nineteen minutes and ten seconds. The critical round was round nine when Cribb struck Molyneux a beautifully timed blow to the head and broke his jaw. Molyneux did not rise to his feet before the statutory thirty seconds. Cribb was dancing a hornpipe around the stage and he could not therefore be declared the winner because the referee could not raise Cribb's right hand to make the victory official, so two more rounds were fought. In round eleven the American champion was felled with a final blow to the head. On the Sunday following the fight Cribb returned to London, his carriage being cheered all the way. He arrived at Holborn on 30 September to a tumultuous reception. A great deal of money was staked on the fight. Cribb received over 1,000 guineas, Molyneux £40! Tom Cribb was idolized as the Champion and only ever fought exhibition fights thereafter. He purchased a public house, The Union Arms, Panton Street, off Haymarket, London. Today it is named after him.

Tom Molyneux was born in 1784 in Virginia and was a slave to wealthy Virginian planter Algernon Molyneux, a landowner and playboy. Algernon's near neighbour John Deyton offered to pit his prize slave against any other slave in a fight with a wager of $100,000. Algernon accepted: he was drunk at the time, but when he sobered up he put Tom into extensive training. Tom won the fight and the vast fortune for his master who granted him his freedom. Tom then took the Molyneux name and became a prize fighter, becoming the champion of America.

An 1890 plan of the site where the Cribb/Molyneux fight took place on 28 September 1811. It is at a point where three counties meet – Leicestershire, Lincolnshire and Rutland. Prize-fighting was illegal but if the magistrates were called from one county to halt a contest, the fighters could move across to the next county. For further information see Dennis Prestidge, *Tom Cribb at Thistleton Gap*, 1976.

EDMONDTHORPE

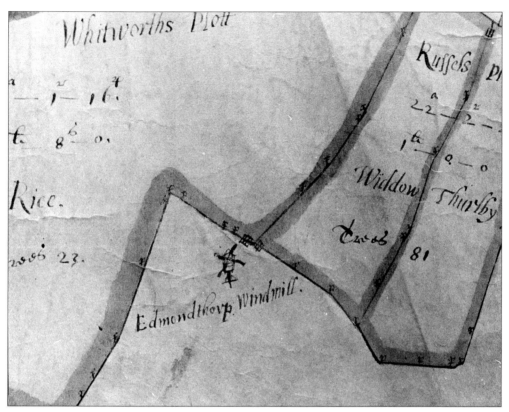

Edmondthorpe windmill on the Sedley estate map of Wymondham, produced in 1652 by Seth Partridge for Sir William Sedley. This windmill stood outside the village off Cord Hill Lane.

Edmondthorpe Hall, 1904. This was the home of Victoria Alexandria, Countess of Yarborough, and John Maunsell-Richardson. The building of the original hall started in 1620; considerable alterations took place in 1700. During the years 1868 to 1869 R.W. Johnson was responsible for designing and building the extensive stables. The hall was burnt down in 1943 while occupied by the army.

The great embankment of the Oakham Canal, off the Teigh Road, Edmondthorpe, 1967. This area has been subjected to an extensive tree-planting scheme and today this view is totally obscured.

The Oakham Canal at Teigh on the boundary between Leicestershire and Rutland, 1967. This head of water is maintained through the construction of an earth dam.

Mile-posts which once stood on the banks of the canal at Edmondthorpe. Left: this post stood near Ellis Lodge and is now resited near Cord Hill Lane. Right: this post was placed in the deep cutting off the Teigh Road, photographed in 1969, and has now been removed by persons unknown!

Roman coins found when the deep cutting was being made in 1790. The navvies dug up a Roman villa. Many artefacts must have been found and when fields on both sides of the cutting are ploughed, pottery roof tiles and hypocaust flues are uncovered.

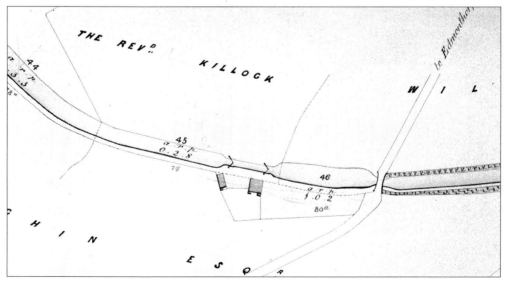

Detail from a plan by Stephen Fry of Lock No. 18 and the lock-keeper's cottage at Edmondthorpe, c. 1850.

Joseph Morley at Stonecroft, Edmondthorpe, *c.* 1900.

Mrs Wyndham, wife of the Hon. Colonel Edward Scawen Wyndham DSO, JP, of Edmondthorpe Hall, riding side-saddle prior to a meet of Cottesmore Hounds in the front of the hall, 1927. A maid from the hall is walking across to the hunters with the stirrup cup.

The Cottesmore Hounds in front of Edmondthorpe Hall, 1927. The master of the foxhounds was James Baird Esq., Huntsman James Welch.

George Marriott milking a cow at Hall Farm, 1935. George had a special relationship with animals. Here he has trained his pet cat to accept cow's milk direct from the teat.

Hall Farm, Edmondthorpe, 1937. Back row, left to right: Florence Marriott, Elizabeth Marriott, Alice Marriott holding a foxcub. Front row: George Marriott holding a foxhound, Tom Marriott. George Marriott farmed out of Hall Farm and at the time this photograph was taken he was raising a foxhound puppy for the Cottesmore Hunt and an orphaned foxcub. They were the best of friends playing together as they grew up. Eventually the hound was taken into the kennels and the fox was released into the wild. It is macabre to think they might have met again in a hunt.

Charlie Barber hedge-laying at Edmondthorpe, 1968, the traditional method of hedge maintenance. When the open fields were enclosed, boundaries were decided by digging ditches; the spoil from the trench was stacked on the landowner's side of the ditch. Into this line of soil were planted sprigs of hawthorne; when it had grown to the height of approximately 4 ft 6 in, it was layered, as is clearly shown in this photograph. Thin lengths of hazel branches were woven along the top, held in place with stakes. Charlie is demonstrating this in the photograph.

CHAPTER THREE

RUTLAND

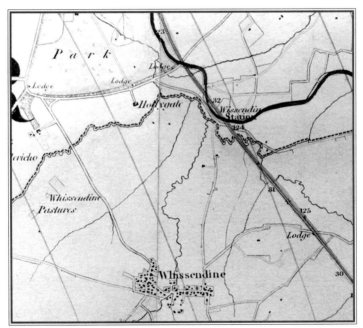

Section of the 1835 edition of the Ordnance Survey, revised in 1867. The Oakham Canal and the Midland Railway are clearly indicated at Whissendine station but this is not an entirely accurate plan: the canal had long since ceased to be functional when this map was revised. As a result of the Battles of Saxby (see p. 67) and the uncompromising attitude of the 6th and last Lord Harborough, attempts were made to construct the railway south of Stapleford Park and the village of Whissendine. The plan was to run the railway through a tunnel under Jericho Hill, passing the village over Whissendine pastures. Work began in 1845 with the digging of the tunnel under Cuckoo Hill plantation. The survey was at fault, the tunnel collapsed, and Lord Harborough sued the railway company for damaging his trees. The outcome of this setback was that the southern line around Stapleford was abandoned and a large curve in the railway was laid out much nearer to the village of Saxby, to the north.

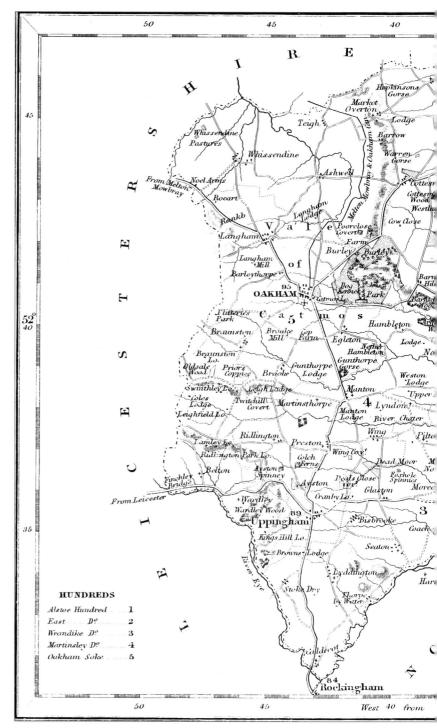

Map of Rutland drawn and engraved by J. Archer, Pentonville, London, 1842. The
Melton Mowbray and Oakham Canal is clearly marked. There are no railways; the
main form of transport was a horse or a horse-drawn vehicle. It is interesting to
note the turnpike roads through Rutland in the 1840s – Melton Mowbray through

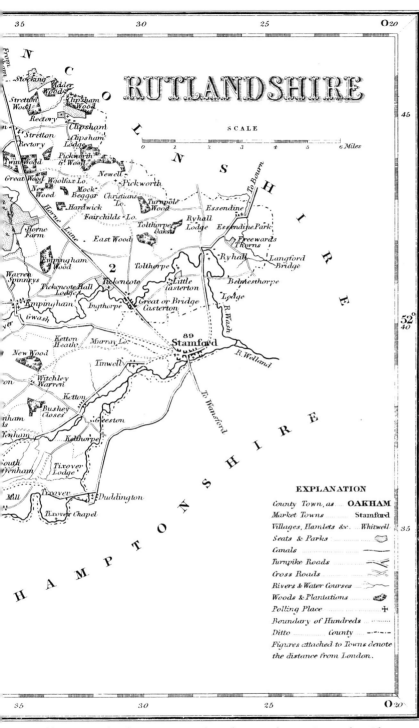

Oakham to Rockingham, Leicester through Uppingham at Barrowden. They were laid through open fields out to Stamford and included the routes from Oakham to Stamford, Oakham to the Great North Road via Cottesmore, Stamford to Bourne and the Great North Road (Horne Lane).

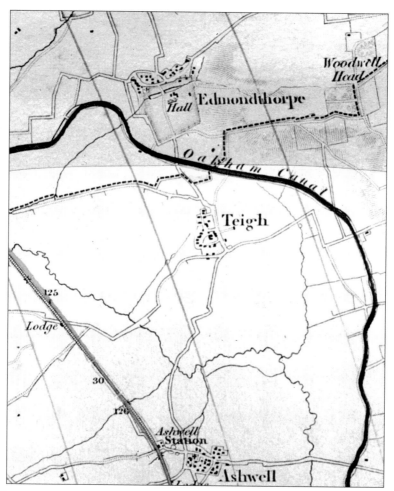

Part of the late nineteenth-century Ordnance Survey map showing the county boundary, Leicestershire and Rutland. The Oakham Canal passed south of the village of Edmondthorpe and to the north-east of Teigh. At the height of the canal trade this area must have been a hive of activity. There was a public house at Edmondthorpe, boats were moored at lock No. 18, and an extensive wharf flourished at Market Overton. Edmondthorpe people have always felt connected to Rutland and for very many years it was a postal district of Oakham. Folklore and legend abound in this district; the story that is perpetuated over the years and into the present century is the tale of the Edmondthorpe witch. In 1655 Sir Roger Smith of Edmondthorpe Hall died. On his monument in the church of St Michael and All Angels are the recumbent figures of his two wives. One, that of Lady Ann Smith, has a red stain on the wrist. She was considered to be a witch who could turn herself into a white cat. During the period that she was living at the Hall as Sir Roger's wife, a white cat was repeatedly caught stealing from the kitchen. This was too much for the cook who attempted to kill it with a cleaver and he cut its paw. Dripping blood, it fled for its life never to be seen again. The next day Lady Ann appeared with a heavily bandaged wrist. Eventually the bandages were removed to leave a red scar. The red mark on the marble effigy in the church is said to bleed at certain times during the year. During the occupancy of Lady Yarborough a flagstone was removed from the hall kitchen because of the permanent red stain that could never be scrubbed off. In 1943 while British soldiers were billeted in the hall the army cook startled a white cat that was stealing food in the kitchen. He threw a rolling pin at it upsetting a candle that fell into a pan of fat and started the disastrous fire. The flames could be clearly seen from the nearby village of Wymondham. The Edmondthorpe witch had had her revenge. The hall was completely gutted and is still a ruin.

TEIGH

THE SPORTS.

PROGRAMME.

EGG & SPOON RACE, for Children under 10 years, 50 yards,
2/- 1/6, 1/- 6d.

FLAT RACE, for Girls between 12 & 15 years, 75 yards,
3/- 2/6, 2/-.

FLAT RACE, for Boys, 150 yards, 2/- 1/-.

FLAT RACE, for Young Men under 25 years, 250 yards, 10/- 5/-.

FLAT RACE, for Women, 60 yards. 1st, Gown Piece; 2nd,
pound of Tea.

FLAT RACE, for Men over 25 years, 75 yards, 6/- 4/- 2/-.

WHEELBARROW RACE open, 50 yards, 5/- 2/6.

THREE-LEGGED RACE, open, 80 yards, 5/- 2/6.

HURDLE RACE, open, 150 yards, 5/- 2/6.

SACK RACE, open, 30 yards, 5/- 2/6.

OBSTACLE RACE, open, 5/- 2/6.

HIGH JUMP, open, 5/- 2/6.

LONG JUMP, open, 5/- 2/6.

Three to run or no race.

The decision of the Judges to be final.

All entries for the Open Races to be made to Mr. BENNETT,
on the ground.

The Committee reserve the right to make any alteration in
the above.

CONCERT.

PROGRAMME.

Part 1.

BELLS .... Edmondthorpe Hand Bells
SONG (Comic) ...... "Muddle Puddle Porter" .. Mr. G. Wormall
SONG (Comic) .... "Up to Dick" .... Mr. E. Eaton
SONG .... Miss Clayton
SONG .... Mr. G. Hack
SONG (Comic) .... Mr. Hoyle
SONG .... "Here, there, and everywhere" .. Mr. H. Morley
DUET (Comic) ...... "Not really" .. Mr. Dawson & Mr. C. Brian
SONG .... Mr. T. Hack

Part 2.

BELLS .... Edmondthorpe Hand Bells
DUET .... "Waves of the ocean" .... The Misses Hill
SONG .... Mr. G. Hack
SONG .... Miss Clayton
SONG (Comic) .. "Right before the Misses too" .. Mr. C. Brian
SONG .... Mr. T. Hack
SONG .... "Dancing round the Apple Tree" .. Mr. Dawson
SONG .... Mr. Hoyle

God Save the Queen.—The Choir.

TEIGH JUBILEE CONCERT AND SPORTS.

June the 8th, 1887.

Teigh is a very small village but it has always been high in community spirit and fund-raising activities, none more ambitious than the programme for the celebrations for Queen Victoria's golden jubilee in 1887.

A village stalwart, George Woolley Morley, aged seventy-eight, feeding goslings and hens at Chestnut Farm, Teigh, 1928.

Laying out sheaves of corn on a stack at Teigh, 1930. Left to right: Mary Tibbs, Joe Morley, Jack Tidd.

Church of the Holy Trinity, Teigh, 1910. As Lord of the Manor the 4th Earl of Harborough instructed the London-based architect George Richardson to redesign part of the village church. He retained the medieval west tower – the lower part is thirteenth and the top part is fourteenth century – but most of the rest of the church was reconstructed and the work began in 1782. The bell frame in the tower is dated 1794. In 1845 the then rector installed the stone font on which he had completed the carvings.

Albert Edward Hudson and Dorothy Leving Gillson on the occasion of their marriage, 20 June 1929.

Evelyn Morley at Yew Tree Farm, 1928. She is washing the top of a butter churn after the weekly butter-making session.

Jack Tidd opening up the stubble with a horse-drawn plough in the First Market Overton field, *c.* 1927.

Jack Tidd on the binder with Bert Tidd and his dog Gip in The Ten Acre, Teigh, 1928. They are cutting the wheat with a horse-drawn binder to produce tied-up sheaves for raising in stacks (*see* bottom right p. 109).

Fred Morley and Jack Tidd with the two Smiths, gathering seed, red clover and rye grass to be dried in a stack then cut up in a chaff-cutter for feeding to horses and cattle, 1927.

A break for tea during haymaking, Teigh, 1927. Left to right: Evelyn and Joseph Morley, Pearl Park and Fred Morley.

The last load of hay, 1934. Left to right: Fred Morley, Bill Cooper, Jack Tidd, Dick Tidd, Rose Morley.

The controversial Vicar of Teigh and friends, *c.* 1930. Left to right: Revd S. Tibbs, Mary Tibbs, Gwen Ellam, Canon Tibbs. Revd Tibbs was a known Fascist.

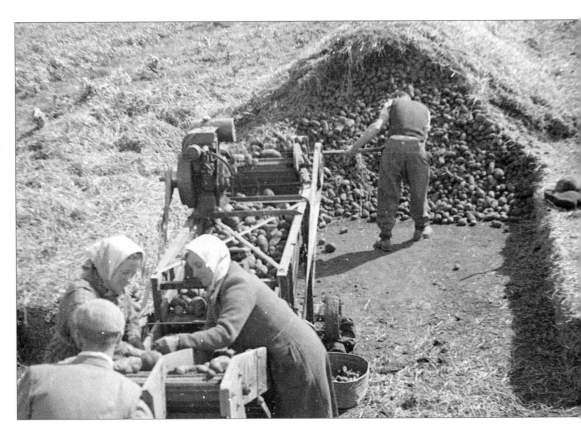

Opening up a clamp of potatoes at Barn Close, Teigh, March 1961. Background: Ray Sykes. Foreground: Gerald Morley, Phyllis Baines, Beatrice Weston.

The famous Rutland Jersey herd of milking cows, parading down the main road to the milking parlour at Teigh. John Cooper bred this fine herd of cattle from his prime cow Honeysuckle (*see* title page).

WHISSENDINE

Main Street, Whissendine, looking east, 1904. The church wall is on the left. The Primitive Methodist church is just visible on the left. The row of cottages (centre background) have been demolished and modern cottages have been erected on the site.

Main Street, Whissendine, looking west, 1904. Stephen Thompson's butcher's shop is on the left with Samuel Coxall's bakehouse a few yards beyond the wooden gate.

Oakham Road, Whissendine, 1905. The highway was little better than a gravel track, with grass growing into the roadway. In the centre stands Whissendine House, the home of Seymour Bouverie (*see* below).

Whissendine House, the home of the Bouverie family, *c.* 1920. In recent years this large house has been developed into smaller units.

St Andrew's church, Whissendine, 1904. The Vicar at the time was the Revd Edward Larkin Horne MA.

Primitive Methodist Chapel, Ashwell Road, *c*. 1920.

SLIPCOAT

A slipcoat mould or press. Wooden cheese-making dishes such as this were used to produce a farmhouse delicacy in Whissendine towards the end of the nineteenth century – unique cheese called Whissendine Slipcoat! Milk was curdled by adding rennet. It was then strained into a vat, so removing the whey, and sufficient curd was placed in a wooden mould. The curd was allowed to drain for around twelve hours until it was firm and was then turned on to a linen cloth and sprinkled with salt, wrapped in cabbage leaves and placed on a shelf in the maturing room, being turned daily for about seven days. The cabbage leaves were replaced after each turning. After one week the cheese was ready for eating. It closely resembled camembert with a similar crust.

The nineteenth-century dairy at Manor Farm, Whissendine, where Ann and William Fowler produced their Slipcoat cheese. For a more detailed account of this cheese consult the *Leicestershire Historian*, Vol. 4, No. 5, 1997.

WHISSENDINE WINDMILL

Whissendine Windmill is a tower mill built of local stone in around 1830. It had ,four patent sails on a Lincolnshire cross. During a violent gale in 1922 the sails were blown off and the cross tree was broken; from that time gradual deterioration set in.

Some repair and maintenance took place and in 1971 a new ogee cap was fitted. In 1995 the mill was purchased by Nigel Moon. Here he checks the flow as it leaves the stones. Using the thumb and forefinger the quality is ascertained, hence the term 'rule of thumb'.

On purchasing the mill Nigel Moon began the long haul to bring it back into production. Power is provided by an electric motor that turns one set of stones. Here Nigel is checking the flow of wheat into the stones.

FORRYAN'S PORK PIES

In 1930 Charles Forryan moved to Whissendine from Melton Mowbray and began to make the traditional Melton Mowbray pork pie in the village. After his death the business continued to flourish under his son John. Today Charles's grandson Warwick still produces prize-winning pork pies in the shop on Main Street. In this photograph Warwick's wife Anne is sealing the lid to the pie case by hand.

Anne Forryan cutting out lids for the hand-raised pork pies. For further reading on the manufacture of the traditional pork pie in this area of England see *The History of the Melton Mowbray Pork Pie*.

Anne Forryan hand-raising the hot water flour pastry around a wooden pie mould. In the foreground are prepared balls of chopped and seasoned pork ready to be placed in the case.

MARKET OVERTON

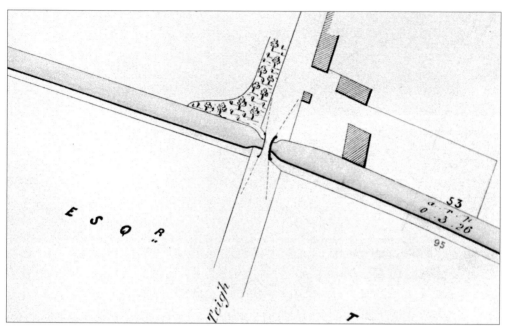

A plan of Market Overton wharf on the Oakham Canal below Market Overton Hill on the Teigh Road,
c. 1850. The large warehouse belonged to the Bennet family who traded out of the yard, mainly in coal.
The small square building just off the bridge was the weighing room and today it still stands off the highway.

The main wharf building standing beside the derelict canal, 1969. This building was possibly used as a
maltings during the life of the canal. The brick wharf can clearly be seen. This was not a canal company
wharf so it was not subject to demolition orders when the canal was sold to the Midland Railway
Company in 1847.

Mrs Gibson's house during the re-slating and general repair of the property, 1950. It is interesting to note that the window above the smithy roof next door was not removed at this time. It had been taken out by the time the photograph below was taken.

The smithy and garage at Market Overton, 1951. The Cottesmore Hounds are meeting on the green near the village stocks. The Master of Foxhounds was Lieutenant Colonel C. Heber-Percy.

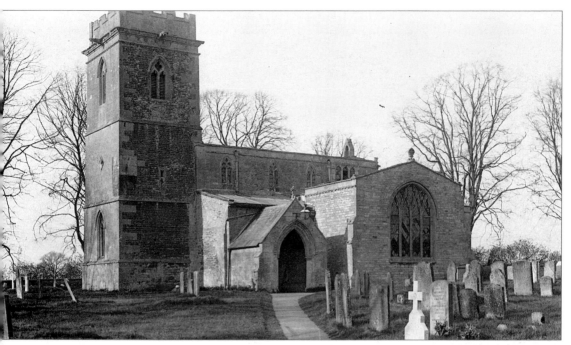

The parish church of St Peter and Paul, 1922. The Vicar at the time was the Revd Robert Edward Jones MA. A Saxon church stood on this site and some of its features are incorporated in the present building. The tower arch is of Saxon origin. Sir Isaac Newton's grandmother is said to have donated the sundial that is positioned on the tower.

Entrance and lych gate to the parish church, *c.* 1922.

BETTY BOOTH

David Cooper and Elizabeth Booth on their wedding day, 1 December 1962. Elizabeth (Betty) Booth was born in Market Overton and was recognized nationally as a highly talented singer. She attended the local school, often singing solos at the school assembly, and on one memorable occasion she stood behind the music stand in front of the whole school and sang 'Blow the Wind Southerly' unaccompanied. When she had finished the headmaster made the comment before the assembled pupils: 'You've got talent. It's time we took your singing seriously.' Arrangements were made with an agency in Leicester and fifteen-year-old Betty travelled every week from Market Overton to Leicester for voice coaching lessons. Her voice developed and the decision was made that Betty should apply to the Royal Academy of Music. She applied, and after an audition she was immediately offered a place at the London college. Betty's career took off, but during holidays she returned to Market Overton and sang with the church choir. The organist was David Cooper: they fell in love and were married. They devoted their lives to singing and Betty travelled the country as a professional performer. Singing controlled her life. Betty Booth reached the pinnacle of her career as a professional singer when she performed solo at the Wigmore Hall, London, on Thursday 4 March 1971. Betty took the stage dressed in an exquisite turquoise evening dress and sang works by Handel, Mahler and Schumann accompanied on the piano by Anthony Saunders. It was a virtuoso performance followed by good reviews in the national press: *Daily Telegraph* – 'Completely musical singing'; *Financial Times* 'Miss Booth sang the songs sympathetically'. The strain of putting on this concert was too great, though, and Betty fell ill. Her career collapsed and David took early retirement to help his wife. A brilliant career came to an abrupt and tragic end.

IRONSTONE MINING

Extensive open-cast mining for iron ore took place around the village of Market Overton. This disrupted agriculture in the area for years. Level-crossings opened overnight; bridges and roads were constructed only to disappear as the face moved on. A Ransome Rapier Dragline is crossing the Thistleton to Market Overton Road in around 1950. There were problems with the position of the overhead telephone wire and the control of traffic. In the foreground stands a GPO van with a police car behind. Fred Hackett is standing in the basket directing proceedings.

No. 5 face, Market Overton open-cast mine, April 1957. In this photograph the dragline illustrated above is shown working on the face.

A Ransome Rapier 5360 Electric Shovel on tracks at the No.6 face in Market Overton Quarry, April 1957.

The Ransome Electric Shovel at work at the No.6 face Market Overton Quarry, one section of the Stewart and Lloyds operation, April 1957.

An extensive Roman villa site uncovered off the Market Overton to Thistleton road after the removal of top soil during open-cast mining operations by Stewart and Lloyds, April 1960. The highly efficient hypocaust system of heating is clearly illustrated. Hot air was conveyed around the villa through a system of flues constructed from box tiles. The heat was supplied from an outside furnace fuelled by wood and the prevailing wind provided the draught. Slaves kept the fire going!

The floors of main living quarters of this villa were decorated with mosaics made up of cut and shaped tiles and decorative stones. The main section shown in this photograph was preserved and used as a wall decoration in Stewart and Lloyds offices at Corby (*see Around Rutland*, p. 58).

BARROW

This sign in Barrow was of a type all too common in most villages in this area. It is still maintained under the eaves on a cottage wall. Note the word 'town' was used: it did not have its modern meaning when the sign was erected and was in fact an adaptation of 'toun', the medieval English term for an enclosed place. The erection of such signs can be traced back to the poor law passed during Elizabeth I's reign (1558–1603). Vagrants had no right to walk on the roads, although it is presumed they could walk the tracks through fields. They were the special concern of the parish constable: unlicensed begging by beggars, vagrants and tramps was a criminal act and according to the law culprits were liable 'to be genuinely whipped and burnt through the right ear'. The normal practice was to whip a vagrant, give him a penny and pass him on to the next village where provisions could be purchased without begging. Large travelling groups could be a real menace and often the militia was called to repel such bands. Sixteenth- and seventeenth-century land clearances by unscrupulous landlords helped create such groups of itinerants. The enclosing of open fields (the communal strip system of farming) to form the fenced grazing fields so typical of these shire counties of today, in some instances resulted in cottage demolition and eviction of many villagers. The evicted became beggars in their own county; congregating together they roamed the countryside looking for work, shelter and above all food. Some would be taken in by sympathetic villagers; some would find work; many would die by the wayside. Such groups could become a menace to a peaceful unsuspecting village and in small villages such as Barrow they could have terrified the resident populace. This old nursery rhyme graphically illustrates such an eventuality:

> Hark! hark! the dogs do bark,
> The beggars are coming to town;
> Some in jags, some in rags,
> And some in velvet gown.
> Some gave them white bread,
> And some gave them brown;
> Some whipped them all soundly,
> And drove them from the town.

COTTESMORE

A Victor coming in to land at RAF Cottesmore, June 1958. In recent decades the countryside around Cottesmore has been dominated by the sound of low-flying military aircraft from the large airfield. Work began on this airfield in 1935. It was a strategic base during the Second World War and was maintained to serve the military during the Cold War period. The first Victor arrived at Cottesmore on 9 April 1958; prior to this the runway had been extended. The Market Overton to Cottesmore road was absorbed into the airfield. This photograph shows a Victor coming in to land over the new roadway that was constructed from Thistleton out to the Great North Road in June 1958. Tornadoes are now stationed at the airfield.

Cottesmore Main Street, 1904. The village green is on the right and the church of St Nicholas is on the left; the vicar at the time was Revd Charles Edward Ellwood.

Remains of an outbuilding on the Oakham Canal Company's wharf at Cottesmore, 1967. In 1840 the company built a cottage to be let to the wharfinger Mr Williamson. Among his duties was responsibility for the canal banks for which he was paid 2s per week. He ran the wharf, part of which was sublet to Mrs Lambert.

Cottesmore wharf toll-keeper's office in ruins, 1967. This drawing is one of Rigby Graham's illustrations for David Tew's book *The Oakham Canal,* Brewhouse Private Press, 1968.

The main street through rural Cottesmore, 1904. Farm workers and the local blacksmith Thomas Hollis are on the right with a pony and trap in the middle distance.

A postcard of Cottesmore House, posted from Oakham as a Christmas card, 1904.

ASHWELL

A general view of the village from the Cottesmore Road, 1904. In the background stands the church of St Mary the Virgin. The Revd Evan Hughes MA was the vicar at the time.

Hugh Crawford with two very fat store pigs at Home Farm, 1935.

Haymaking at Home Farm, Ashwell, 1935. The workers are resting after gathering up the hay with a sweep and rake. Standing, left to right: George Brewster, Richard Fryer, -?-, Hugh Crawford, Ted Tomblin. Seated: -?-, Sidney Brewster, -?-.

Shooting party at Ashwell Hall,1935. Standing, left to right: George Fryer, -?-, Billy Crawford, Colonel Frederick Blair (owner of the Hall), Archie Crawford, -?-, William Crawford, -?-. Kneeling: Hugh Crawford, John Crawford, Jack Crawford, Bob Rippin.

Tom Wright ploughing with Trip and Trixie, Ashwell, 1938.

Ashwell Cricket Club, 1934. Back row, left to right: Albert Ofield, Bob Rippin, Harry Grice, -?-, George Brewster, Umpire ? Front row: Arthur Towns, -?-, Hugh Crawford, Major Herbert Whalley, -?-, -?-, Bill Ellis.

Old Hall, Ashwell, the home of Sir Henry Bromley, Bart, JP, 1904.

Ashwell Lodge, the home of Captain Herbert Whaley, 1916.

Wash day, Ashwell, 1922.

Cottesmore Hunt kennels on the Wymondham road at Ashwell, 1967. These kennels were built in 1889 for the sum of £6,777 by Hollis of Cottesmore and were opened on 5 November 1890 with hunting the next day. William Bird was Master of Foxhounds. At the time this photograph was taken the MFH and Huntsman was Major Robert Hoare.

LANGHAM

Well Street, Langham, 1916. The church of SS Peter and Paul is in the background. The Revd William Alfred Mandell MA was vicar at the time.

Thatched cottages on the Cold Overton Road, Langham, 1935.

Langham School,1932. Behind the school is the Noel Arms public house. The landlord was George Davie, who also ran the garage, petrol pumps and car hire business. To the right is the Wheatsheaf public house, landlord Cecil James Hill.

Morris dancers at the Noel Arms public house, Langham, 1989.

BARLEYTHORPE

Barleythorpe, 1916. The Earl of Lonsdale DL, JP was residing at the Hall.

Peter Jackson and Frank Slavin fighting for the championship of the British Empire at the National Sporting Club, London, 1892. Peter Jackson, of West Indian extraction, was the winner. Peter was a familiar figure running on the Barleythorpe highways as part of his training. He also used Lord Lonsdale's excellently equipped gymnasium, staying at the Hall as the Earl's guest. Lonsdale was known as the 'Yellow' Earl, a nickname he earned by dressing his stewards in the colour and always wearing a yellow flower in his lapel. This drawing by Rigby Graham is taken from Tom Langley's book *The Life of Peter Jackson, Champion of Australia*, 1974.

BURLEY ON THE HILL

The Hall, 1922. During this year the house was let to Rt Hon. Captain Frederick Edward CBE, DSO, MP, Secretary of State for Air.

Sir Jeffrey Hudson, height 1 ft 6 in, Rutland's famous 'Knight in Miniature'. Born in Oakham in 1619, he just did not grow. When he was about nine years old his father, who worked on the estate at Burley on the Hill, introduced the little boy to the then owner, the Duke of Buckingham. King Charles I and Queen Henrietta Maria were guests of the Duke and, as a surprise for part of the evening's entertainment, Jeffrey was dressed in armour, placed in a pie dish and a baked pie crust was placed over him. The pie was served up in front of the King; out jumped Jeffrey scattering crust and crumbs over the royal couple. Much to the amazement and delight of the assembled guests, Jeffrey danced around the table jabbing his small sword at the lighted candles. The Queen requested Jeffrey join the royal court and he was made a Knight shortly after. He had many adventures not least of all charging Cromwell's army at the Battle of Newbury at the side of Prince Rupert. The royalists retreated with the Roundheads shouting after them 'There goes Prince Rupert and Cock Robin!' (see *A Celebration of Rutland*, p. 67).

Burley House after the disastrous fire of 6 August 1908.

One of the highlights of the agricultural year in Rutland is the Rutland County Show that is held annually at the end of May each year in front of Burley House. Here we see the final parade of the day's entertainment, including the supreme champion bull, in the main show ring, 1990s.

The thatched barns of Little Pound Farm, Burley, 1920s.

The Hermitage, a thatched summer house in Burley woods, 1920s.

CHAPTER FOUR

OAKHAM

King Edward VII died in 1910 and was mourned by the nation. In Oakham Castle a tribute was hung to him. It was a garland in the shape of a horseshoe, so appropriate in the historic setting of the Great Hall, where many horseshoes have been deposited, some by long dead monarchs. Any peer of the realm that passes through Oakham is requested to present a horseshoe to the Lord of the Manor; it is then hung in the castle. In Around Rutland the author offers his theory on how that tradition began.

The Boat Inn, Ashwell Road, Oakham, 1983. This former pub is now a private house. Note the small window behind the gate; this was a hatch that was opened to serve ale to the users of the wharf on the canal at the rear of the property.

Oakham station,1904. Robert Herbert was the stationmaster at the time. The building was opened on 1 May 1848.

OAKHAM CASTLE

The Great Hall, Oakham Castle, with the backdrop of the famous horseshoes. Oakham Castle is the home of the County Assize Court.

In January 1996 another functional use of the Great Hall was devised. Many weddings are now held here.

POLO GROUND

The Polo Ground, off Melton Road, Oakham, *c*. 1914. An aircraft has made an emergency landing and repairs are being undertaken prior to take off.

Inspection of the Rutland Volunteers Regiment by Field Marshal Lord French on the Polo Ground, Oakham, 13 May 1917.

HIGH STREET

High Street, Oakham, *c.* 1916. In the centre background is Freeman, Hardy and Willis Ltd, boot makers.

High Street and the Crown Hotel. This picture was probably taken in around 1941 when Mrs V.A. Barnacle was the proprietress.

County Cinema, High Street, Oakham, early 1950s. The film being shown at the time was *Silver City* starring Randolph Scott. Building work started on this cinema in 1939. It was opened on Friday 27 September 1940 as the Regent, closed on 9 July 1988, and was demolished.

Northgates, Oakham, 1960.

OAKHAM MARKET

Buttercross and stocks in the Market Place, Oakham, 1930s. The cross and stocks were erected in the seventeenth century. Dairy products were sold weekly on this site; local cheeses such as Stilton, Slipcoat and Red Leicester were always on offer.

Market Square, Oakham, *c.* 1910. The shops in the background are, left to right: Pascall, chemist; Smith, grocer; J.T. Perkins, general dealer; G.E. Barnett, butcher.

CUTTS CLOSE

Bandstand and paddling pool, Cutts Close, during the Second World War.

Aerial view of Cutts Close, c. 1940. The Old School (centre), an Elizabethan building, was converted into the Shakespeare Centre – Oakham School's theatre – and opened by John Jerwood on 25 October 1969. The opening was celebrated by staging the Malvolio story from *Twelfth Night*.

Church of All Saints and Oakham Castle, a very popular photographic view taken in the late 1930s.

Modern Oakham, the Mill Street roundabout from the air, 1990s.

The Market Place, Oakham, 1950s.

A corner of the Market Place, Oakham, 1960.

THE GEORGE HOTEL

The George Hotel, the Market Place, Oakham, 1941. Charles T. Adey was the proprietor.

George 'Scuttles' Burton in the tap room at the George Hotel, 1960.

The George Hotel, 1960.

Catmose, the residence of Major Henry Cecil Noel JP, 1915. It is now Rutland County Council's offices.

HM Queen Elizabeth II signing the visitors book on Oakham School playing field, 1964. She attended a ceremony to dedicate an ambulance for the disabled in the County of Rutland.

The Vicarage, 1910. It was the home of the Revd James Hamilton Charles MA, rural dean of Rutland.

Fritham House, Oakham School Junior School, 1915. The housemaster was Sidney Sweetman MA.

OSIER BASKETS

Before the canals were dug across the English countryside the main method of transporting goods for centuries was by pack-horse trains. Goods were carried in wicker baskets, strapped to the side of each animal. Here at the Old House Gallery, Oakham, Suki Pryce is weaving a basket from willow in the time-honoured fashion.

Baskets made from locally grown willow and dogwood. Osier beds were scattered along the Eye valley and the Vale of Catmose at the time when the Oakham Canal was dug. Bundles of willow branches from the osier beds were transported from this area on the canal to the industrial Midlands. A few overgrown beds still survive. To maintain the beds, the fast-growing willow must be cut down each autumn, otherwise it develops into large bushy growths, covered with 'pussy willow' catkins in the spring.

Cold Overton Road, the highway leading into Oakham from the west, *c.* 1950.

Uppingham Road, leading into Oakham from the south, *c.* 1930.

CHINA COLLECTABLES

Two pottery souvenirs from Rutland. On the left is a model of a Roman pot found at Ifold Villa, Painswick, Gloucestershire, in 1902. It was manufactured by the Stoke-on-Trent potter W.H. Goss. On the right is the Jeffrey Hudson teapot modelled and made by Richard Parrington, Collectors Teapots, Whitstable, Kent, for Colin Holden of Acorn Antiques in the Market Place, Oakham.

Entrance to the Market Place, High Street, Oakham, c. 1955.

ACKNOWLEDGEMENTS

The compilation of the text and the selection of the illustrations for this book was made possible through the encouragement given to the author by his father John Cecil Hickman and his mother Elsie May Hickman, who showed him how to appreciate the countryside of north-east Leicestershire and to be aware of man's involvement in creating the rural landscape of this part of England. Rigby Graham showed the way to place apparently unimportant features of the landscape into their true perspective and David Tew's researches enabled this book to be compiled. Many people have offered advice and encouragement and have of course provided many unrecorded facts that are published in this book for the first time. To the following the author offers his sincere thanks: Eileen Andrew, Anne Bridgman, John Cooper, Jill Gregg, Lady Jennifer Gretton, Ian Manchester, Sheila Manchester, Helen Mapletoft, Audrey Morley, George Morley, Pippa Morris, Gwen Mutch, Michael Neal, Mel Price, Walter Skerritt, Daphne Adine Toulson, Richard Warner, Tim Williams, John Wright, and Pat Peters for typing the author's manuscript for the publisher's use.

Permission has been granted to publish the photographs and illustrations reproduced in this book. If, however, through an oversight by the author any photographs should be reproduced without permission, Trevor Hickman offers his sincere apologies and will make due acknowledgement in future editions.

The end of the beginning! In this photograph taken in around 1905 three children are sitting or standing on the drain that was laid along the bed of the canal before it was filled in. The cutting left the River Wreake and continued across what is now the Play Close to the basin on Burton End and then on to Oakham.

LIST OF PLACES & FEATURES

When Burton Street, Melton Mowbray, became a canal, Bank Holiday Monday 8 August 1922.